recover
your
balance

HOW TO BOUNCE BACK FROM BAD TIMES AT WORK

ANN LEWIS

First Published as 'Getting Back On Track'
in Canada by Trafford Publishing 2008

This Edition published in Great Britain by
Bookshaker (www.bookshaker.com) 2010

For Peter, my rock and best friend.

CONTENTS

PRAISE

"Brilliant book! Just what I needed, exactly when I needed it. I had to have my own copy, it's the kind of book that I revisit over and over again. Each time I see something from a different view. Thank you so much for taking the time to write it."

Kim Eagletone M.Inst.S.R.M.Dip., M.I.L.A.M

"This book with its warm and human, but clear and purposeful, approach is a great morale booster for those going through difficult times. It helps build personal effectiveness and maintain a sense of perspective when things can seem bleak."

Ros Cassy, development consultant

"Ann's book has had a phenomenal impact on clients of mine who have read it. When Ann works with you she is not only professional but she is one of the few people who truly connects with you on all levels."

Salma Ismail, Owner, Grassroots Consulting:
www.grassrootsconsulting.co.uk

"Do you need 2 regain your confidence & control at work? Have a look at this by @annlewiscoach. Great advice and tips."

Sharon Gaskin, The Trainers' Training
Company (posted on twitter.com)

"As a coach, Ann is attentive, insightful and thorough. Her programme and book evolved from real personal experience. Ann truly understands what inner resources people need to reframe and rebuild their confidence and their lives."

Penny Millar, owner, photoVoyage:
www.photovoyage.co.uk

"A small book that packs a mighty punch; re-reading Ann's book reminded me that I should have done this a few months ago during a particularly bad spell of bullying at work. The lessons learnt from previous sessions with Ann and my first reading of her book gave me the strength to understand what was happening and stop it.

"The negative thoughts and lack of inner self-confidence that I experienced are described with uncanny accuracy and understanding – the self coaching to take charge and change has really worked for me. Thank you."

Sylvia, former client – Senior Manager, Healthcare

"This book offers amazing resources for everyone - Ann provides clear wisdom and insights about the difficult challenges we're all facing, as well as tangible tools and techniques to make those powerful, positive changes you've been wishing for!"

Dr. Daniel Scott, author of Verbal Self Defense in the Workplace, www.verbalselfdefensebook.com

ACKNOWLEDGEMENTS

Many people have helped this book into existence. My thanks go to Gareth, Karen, Laura, Lou, Nicola, Rebecca, Rob, Sarah, Sue and Truus, (not their real names), who generously took the time to tell me their stories, gave me their blessing to include them here, and read and commented on the first draft. You know who you are, and your contributions have made the book real.

The experiences of many of my coaching clients suggested that a way to *Recover Your Balance* was needed. Thank you for the opportunity to work with you and through that work, to lay the foundations for the book. My creative coach AnnA Rushton was with me from the start, encouraging me to find my voice, egging me on and sharing some brilliant tea shops and pubs in East Sussex. Judy Oliver and friends in ANKLe (A New Kind of Leadership) made a workshop possible to test some of the ideas. Authors Nancy Kline and Susan Debnam were supportive and encouraging. Martha Leyton meticulously edited the first edition manuscript. Debbie Jenkins and the Publishing Academy team who brought the second edition into being and showed me how to get it to a much bigger readership.

Developing as a coach has also been part of my own journey to Recover *My* Balance. Thanks to the Academy of Executive Coaching, especially Marion Gillie (who asked the crucial question), John Leary Joyce and my coaching buddies Eileen Arney, Eversley Felix and Liz Walmsley. I've also loved working with and being challenged by colleagues Lindsay Wittenberg, Carole Pemberton, Miriam Orriss, Martin Shovel and Martha Leyton, Stephen Burt, Kate Harmond, and Nancy Kline and the Time to Think coaching and mentoring community.

And of course, my husband Peter, who has encouraged endlessly, shown the patience of a saint, and brought a welcome touch of silliness when I needed it most, as well as my Mum and Dad, who amaze me daily.

FOREWORD

Reading this book is almost like being with Ann herself. And that is a gift. Ann's astute, practical, inspiring expertise as a coach comes alive in these pages. We experience her warmth, her encouragement, her genuine honouring of us, in every word. Our minds open to the positive truths about ourselves and to the exciting possibilities we can create.

These pages resound with warranted optimism.

Ann's understanding of the psychology of discouragement grounds her positive approach and she helps lift us out of even the most demoralising circumstances. And her understanding of energy states gives us a concrete, rich context in which to understand and reclaim our true selves at three important levels.

Also, we easily identify with the key characters in her narratives and enjoy the ingenious way she has threaded the stories of the characters through the key points and the process. The efficacy of the process stands tall against the concrete practical results the characters have experienced in practice.

I am drawn to Ann's work and to this book because it puts into action one of my most cherished values: the right of each person to think for themselves. Ann does this by creating what I call a Thinking Environment. And within that safe, stimulating, respectful space, Ann invites us to do our own thinking. She asks us questions. They are clear, sharp, requiring depth and authenticity of reflection. They also are concretely affirming of us and our talents, strengths, values, joys and successes.

Perhaps the most important message in this book is: "You are in charge. You have choice. You are not a victim. You can understand yourself, your life, your situation. And you can design your future."

Ann demonstrates compellingly that without question the best is yet to come.

If you can get Ann to be your coach, do. If you can't, let her change your life through this book.

Better still, do both.

Nancy Kline, author of
'Time to Think' and 'More Time to Think'
www.timetothink.com

INTRODUCTION

There is a taboo in the workplace. I call it 'alright-ism'. We seem unable or unwilling to acknowledge and take control of experiences at work that sap our confidence, lower our self-esteem and batter our resilience. Things can be really going pear-shaped, and we still feel obliged to say 'it's alright' because to say anything else feels like failure, and failure is too painful to admit. Not only that, we fear the response of those around us, who may get nervous or condemn our faintheartedness. So we deny the pain and carry on. I think it's time to break the taboo.

When your confidence and self-esteem disappear, fear, anger, distress and other negative emotions come into play. These in turn distort the way you see the world, and your responses to it. You may find it hard to trust anyone around you. The innocent remarks and everyday actions of other people take on a sinister appearance. You wake with anxiety in your heart, and it grows during the day. You are forever, metaphorically, looking over your shoulder. You may worry about taking any time off, even leave to which you're entitled, for fear of what may be waiting for you when you go back. The problem can overshadow your every waking hour.

There is growing evidence that negative emotions seriously hamper your effectiveness. That on which you dwell grows stronger. If you focus on the negative, you increase its power over you. You also project this negative energy all the time, within yourself and to those around you. Without necessarily being aware of it, people feel dragged down by negativity, and may take steps to avoid being sucked into it. Friends begin to distance themselves, leaving their space to others who prefer to fuel your negative energy.

If you are being bullied, your bully can unconsciously pick up the fear and anxiety you project when they are around you. This increases their sense of power to harm you. If you are worried about a situation, your worry can seriously hamper your ability to deal effectively with it. If you lack confidence, your timidity prevents you from facing and taking charge of your situation.

As a coach I have come across many bright, capable people who go through a distressing experience at work and do not share it with anyone because of their fears of what others will think, and of how they will be perceived. They feel isolated with the problem, and it causes huge distress. If you have experienced such distress this book is written for you.

If your confidence is compromised by what is going on in your working life, you can do something about it, and you can emerge stronger. You may not be able to change the circumstances, but you can choose how you respond to them.

Recover Your Balance acts as a virtual coach, encouraging you back towards self-belief, confidence and the positive emotions that will fuel a full recovery and literally help you 'recover your balance'. You will understand what is going wrong, and get really clear about what you want from the situation and from your life. And you can start taking action right now to recover your self-belief and effectiveness. I will show you how.

The Story Behind Recover Your Balance

The seeds of *Recover Your Balance* were sown early in my career. At the time, I worked as a personnel administrator and managed a small team. Now, I confess that administration is not my forte. I do it, but I don't love it. I'm not passionate about it. Looking back, I can say without any doubt that I was in the wrong job.

Overall, I made a passable stab at the work, learned a lot, and did my best to make small dents in my company's traditional, subtly sexist culture. I was young, quite bright and capable, fairly insecure, appreciative of the abilities of my team, and acutely aware of being a woman in a very macho environment not long after the UK Sex Discrimination Act became law.

One day, out of the blue, my boss's PA asked to fix a meeting between myself and him for that same evening, when most other people would have gone home. I queried the time, but was offered no flexibility, so I cancelled a personal appointment and complied with the request. I wonder now why I did not immediately smell a rat.

To my complete shock, at the meeting my boss read out a list of misdemeanours he said I had committed, which had never before been aired, and threatened me with dismissal if I ever made another mistake. Only two or three months before he'd given me a very positive appraisal. Now I was suddenly faced with a final warning (interestingly, never written down).

Following an unsuccessful appeal, after which my Staff Council representative declared that he had never seen anyone quite so comprehensively stitched up, I spent the next few months trying to be absolutely perfect, an endeavour doomed to failure. My daily routine included vomiting every morning before I left home. Finally, after taking a couple of days leave, I returned to find that a part of my team's work had been very publicly passed around to other people's PAs in an attempt to demonstrate that I was failing. I resigned. For more than two years afterwards I simply didn't believe that I was worthy of a well-paid job with similar status to the one I had left.

My family and close friends were unswervingly supportive, and must have suffered hugely from my distress. However, they were not impartial, and I was completely blameless in their eyes. This polarisation of opinion made it difficult to look at the situation dispassionately and find the learning. With hindsight, I believe that coaching, had it existed, would have made a substantial difference to how I coped.

I did eventually find my balance again, and the seeds of *Recover Your Balance* germinated over the years as I worked with many managers to help them treat their people fairly and consistently. Even when poor performance is managed sensitively and fairly, people still feel vulnerable, and this must be acknowledged. The seedling became a heavily disguised 'how not to do it' case study. However, I was aware of the shadow of this experience on occasion, even years later.

Real People, Real Experiences

After I became a coach, I began to meet and support people whose work circumstances had also knocked them off balance in a variety of ways. Each one was completely different, but the effects were strikingly similar – feelings of suspicion and mistrust, damaged confidence and battered self-esteem. Like me, they found it hard to talk about what was happening. One of my clients described emerging from her experience "in remarkably good shape". One major difference between her experience and mine was that she had a coach.

Many of my early *Recover Your Balance* clients were women. Interestingly, when I began to talk more about my work, it was often men who sought me out to tell me about their experiences. Their stories are all too typical: Bill, whose company was taken over, and who was frozen out of his dream job; David, who was bullied out of his management role when he challenged a badly designed administrative system on behalf of his frustrated team; Adam, whose new overseas bosses pushed him close to a nervous breakdown.

One of them asked me, "How do you get men, who are supposed to be tough and tolerant of stress, even to admit they have a problem?" I've wondered about this myself, and my working theory is that specific help in such situations has been hard to find, and talking to colleagues and friends feels very risky. The same is true for women, of course, but we are more willing, on the whole, to notice and talk about our feelings.

The stories in this book are all genuine. They come from people, my clients and others, who have gone through, and recovered from, some really challenging and difficult events at work. Without them the book would be poorer.

Your Call to Action

Please know this: you are a fully functioning human being who is temporarily off balance. You have some strengths and some weaknesses. Everyone does. You are not alone. Whatever else anyone tries to tell you, you are worthy of as much respect and dignity as every other human being. Eleanor Roosevelt famously said: "No-one can make you feel inferior without your consent." This book is about helping you to inhabit again the fully functioning persona you had before all this happened, and with the bonus of greater awareness and resilience. There is a life after your current difficulties, and you are going to create it.

Let's begin.

Ann Lewis

CHAPTER ONE

ENERGY & PRESENCE – THE FOUNDATIONS

*I do think that one of the real issues is the
pressure on you to be successful in a job, and
to make it work. You sometimes put up with so
much because of that pressure. And then we
don't stop and think 'well, what is important to
me, what do I need to do to make this better?'*
Lou

You spend a huge proportion of your waking life
at work. When things are going well, work can
be fulfilling and enjoyable. However, when you
are off balance, it can be a misery. Let's begin by
looking at what can knock you off balance. Then
we'll explore how to work with your energy to
break the spell and get you moving again.

The Triggers That Knock You Off Balance

Experiences that lead to a loss of balance include
both the personal and the organisational.

Personal triggers may include:

- being bullied
- a difficult relationship with a boss
- a colleague's actions that challenge your own ethical standards
- being under-resourced or under-skilled for the work in hand
- being in the wrong job
- the failure of a major customer's business
- recovery from illness

Organisational triggers include:

- constant, ill-thought-through change
- poorly managed takeovers and mergers
- redundancy or business failure
- poor communication
- economic constraints that limit promotion opportunities
- corporate values that clash with yours and result in your ignoring or suppressing your own values

You're Not Alone – Sharing Real Experiences

Along the way we'll follow the experiences of others who have been where you are now, and benefit from their wisdom and insight to see how they coped and overcame their setbacks – people like Gareth, Lou, Rob, Nicola, Laura and others. Here are some of their triggers:

Nicola deputised for a senior manager in a major public sector organisation, and enjoyed a close and positive relationship with her boss. She says: "About a year into the job, (my boss) went on a long holiday and left me in charge. There were several high profile and unpredictable problems, which reached the national media. I handled these as well as I could, and on (my boss's) return some of the senior staff met with her and told her how much they appreciated my efforts. One of our most 'challenging' managers e-mailed widely, praising my decisions and behaviour.

"From then on, she froze me out. She avoided meeting with me alone and blocked my calls. I was assigned a new area of responsibility, which did not fit my skill set or personal style. I felt I was being set up to fail in a very public way and could not work out why."

Rob worked in a nurse specialist role in an NHS Trust. "The Trust was overspent and they were looking at ways to save money. The hospital management committee had a series of meetings to look for possible cost saving initiatives.

"One of the hospital consultants, who had very little to do with the work I was doing was calling for the withdrawal of funding for my role. My boss was less than supportive and simply highlighted that this was a possibility, without suggesting possible solutions or ways to 'fight' this decision should the need arise."

Lou was Human Resources Director with a non-profit organisation. A change of Chief Executive turned a job she loved into a demoralising treadmill. She says: "There was no development going on at this time – it was all about resolving issues in the top team. Imagine how that was going down in the organisation. It was just dire. And the thing I loved about my job was the development opportunities for getting people really reaching their potential. I wasn't doing any of that. I was firefighting the whole of the time, trying to support people's self-esteem, making them feel good, and actually, what about my self-esteem? I felt (I was) nothing – absolutely nothing. This guy would just dismiss me."

Gareth is a designer. When the business of a major client began to fail, it took him a while to realise what was happening, as the true situation was glossed over. Eventually the client's business was wound up, but the available assets were used to pay outstanding tax. Gareth says: "The real creditors, people like myself who had supplied goods and services got nothing. The client owed me in the region of GBP30,000 which even now would be significant, but in 1992 it was devastating."

Laura was Chief Executive of a large, complex NHS organisation, which she led through a difficult merger. She says: "Whilst the organisation was making great progress on winning staff and the public over to change, the view from the centre was that our performance on money and waiting lists was not robust enough. The then Regional CEO put pressure on my Board for me to leave and effectively they had no option. Many senior clinicians and staff as well as Local Authority colleagues protested, to no avail."

Energy – The Key To Recovering Your Balance

Whatever the cause, when you're off balance, your energy is compromised on all levels, and getting it properly functioning is the key to feeling fully alive again.

For Rob "Work became unbearable. First it was difficult to get up in the mornings and then Sunday evenings became a part of the weekend I dreaded, and Friday evenings the focus for the week. Everything about my job started to get me down and I found even the most minor problem or criticism impossible to cope with."

Laura told me: "I felt under siege, very emotional and extremely angry! It has taken several years to work through all of that and to regain my self confidence and equilibrium."

Reflecting on her experience, Nicola says: "I suppose my message is about understanding that any loss – whether of confidence, status, intimacy or respect – is a type of bereavement. The same cycles of denial, numbness, guilt, anger, despair, hurt and acceptance apply – but this is not a linear process and the phases will be repeated."

Lou says, "Then it came to one weekend... I knew I had to face him. I had to face the way he was treating me... I knew I was going to have to have a head-to-head. And every time I thought about it, I kept crying. I was very emotionally unstable, basically, I was crying at everything, and I felt awful."

How you experience and use energy is critical to your health and wellbeing. So how does *Recover Your Balance* talk about energy?

Two key concepts appear throughout the book:

1. Energy States, which relate directly to your Presence in the world, and

2. Energy Dimensions, the physical, emotional, mental and spiritual aspects of your energy.

Presence & The Flow Of Energy – Understanding Energy States

In *Presence – How To Use Positive Energy For Success*[1], Patsy Rodenburg develops her theory of three core energy states - she calls them Three Circles of Energy - that describe how our energy connects with that of others, and how we show up in the world. Each energy state is reflected through each of the four energy dimensions, and affects how people experience us and how we function. Rodenburg's work as Director of Voice for London's Guildhall School of Music and Drama, along with her years at the Royal National Theatre and the Royal Shakespeare Company give her a holistic

---

[1] *The Second Circle* US edition

perspective on how body, mind, emotions and spirit interact, and how Presence can be intentionally accessed. Throughout *Recover Your Balance,* we'll refer to these three energy states. Here is a brief description of them.

First State[2] – Inwardly Focused, Withdrawing

In this energy state, your focus is inward. Physically you may be hunched in on yourself, breathing shallowly, averting your gaze from others and often inaudible when you speak. Others may ignore you, some may be tempted to bully you, and you will have difficulty in asserting yourself or getting your needs met. You may tend towards self-consciousness, feeling insecure, fearful, tentative or uncertain. Your thinking may be clouded by fear or anxiety. If you're off balance, as in your current situation, you may well find that you sometimes retreat into First State. Here, you're vulnerable to bullying and other forms of abuse.

Second State[3] - Present

The core of your work in *Recover Your Balance* is about understanding and accessing your Presence, i.e. that state in which you are fully

---

[2] Adapted from Rodenburg's 'First Circle'

[3] Adapted from Rodenburg's 'Second Circle'

alive and alert in the moment, able to connect on an equal footing with those around you, open to hearing accurately what others say without leaping to judgment, and able to focus fully on whatever you are doing.

Second State is your natural state, the place where you are most yourself. Physically you are balanced, breathing fully and quietly. Your body is alert and at ease. You are able to connect fully and appropriately with others. When you walk into a room you'll be noticed in a positive way. You will be fully aware of the world around you, whether your focus is on your work in all its aspects, a country walk, a sporting event, a piece of art or music, conversation or food, a book or a beautiful sunset.

As you increasingly recover your balance, you'll be accessing Second State readily and naturally.

Third State[4] – Pushing Against, Forceful

Have you noticed how some people seem to take up far more space than others, not so much in terms of size, but through sheer forcefulness? In Third State, you may breathe, speak and move too loudly. Your body will be tensed and your chest forced up and out. You'll habitually look

---

[4] Adapted from Rodenburg's 'Third Circle'

past the person you're talking to, shout to get what you want and send people into retreat from you. This is the state from which bullies, tyrants and even some 'jobsworths' operate. Unfortunately it is also the dominant state that underpins traditional Western male conditioning which can carry through into many organisational cultures. Authentic leaders operate in Second State, not in Third. From Third State, a bully will sense a victim in First State and react accordingly. Second State energy does not attract similar abuse. You may also operate from Third State if you are anxious, defending yourself against events that you experience as attacking.

Presence is accessed only in Second State. However, you need to be able to access all three energy states. For example, in an unfamiliar street at night, you may want to be fully alert in Second, but appear withdrawn into first to avoid attracting attention. Or you may need to put up a barrier (in Third State) to deter unwanted intrusion into your physical or energy space.

We generally operate in all three states at different times, but tend towards a dominant one. Listening, breathing, speaking, feeling and thinking all differ with our Energy State, and awareness is important to recovering your balance effectively.

I've called the three Energy States 'First', 'Second' and 'Third' throughout the book. Please feel free to rename them if a particular metaphor, colour or other descriptive word brings them alive for you. This might be especially helpful with First and Third States.

- What is your dominant energy state?

- When does it serve you and when does it work against you?

- What are your own names for the three Energy States?

If you would like to learn more about energy states, I thoroughly recommend that you read Patsy Rodenburg's book[5], which contains a wealth of insight and useful exercises.

Energy Dimensions

The journey through *Recover Your Balance* moves through the four energy dimensions, starting by paying attention to the physical. Here they are in summary:

- **Physical energy:** is about how you feel in your body, and what physical effects may be linked to being off balance, for

---

[5] Rodenburg, Patsy, *Presence (US: The Second Circle)*, Penguin Books.

example, feeling sick, tenseness in your shoulders, insomnia. Your physical energy is closely intertwined with your emotional energy, and research shows[6] that an imbalance in the emotions directly impacts on the body.

- **Emotional energy:** in this context, we will look at the toxic effect of the negative emotions you may be feeling, both on your ability to function and on your physical health, and find ways to generate positive emotional energy.

- **Mental energy:** refers to the quality of your thinking, your ability to focus appropriately, and your level of optimism or pessimism.

- **Spiritual energy:** is about your sense of a strong purpose in life, passion and commitment, and any connection you may feel to a power and energy larger than yourself, whatever you may call it.

---

[6] See Pert, Candace, *Molecules of Emotion,* Simon & Schuster, and Janssen, Thierry, *La Solution Intérieure,* Fayard

Seven Steps To Recover Your Balance

From now on, we'll look at how physical, emotional, mental and spiritual energies interplay and how you can raise each and all of them, harnessing their positive aspects to get you moving forward again. Your different energies are inter-related, and all are important. You'll see how each Energy Dimension is affected by your Energy State. In your seven steps to getting yourself back in balance, you'll be working on each of them, and building a firm foundation from which to go forward. Here's how it will work:

STEP	PURPOSE	ENERGY FOCUS
1: The dynamics of distress (chapter 2).	Gaining an understanding of being off balance.	Physical, emotional and mental – setting the scene.
2: Understanding where you are and deciding where you're going (chapter 3).	Envisioning a positive outcome; getting grounded. Developing passion for the future and building your self-worth. Understanding objectively what is happening; examining your responses; relating to yourself; relating to others.	Physical: internal physical systems (understanding and influencing the wider physical effects of emotional states). Building a physical foundation. Emotional: connecting emotional and physical energy.
3: Reconnecting with yourself (chapter 4).	Understanding who you are. Looking at your strengths, successes, your personal power and self-esteem.	Emotional: Regenerating positive emotions towards yourself and your place in life.
4: Reflecting for the future (chapter 5).	Accepting yourself as you are. Learning from this experience. Honouring yourself enough to do this.	The boundary between phy-sical/emot-ional and mental/sp-iritual. Self-acceptance and learning.

5: Moving on (chapter 6).	Bringing your future vision to life. Thinking through your plan. Expressing your intentions and needs. Getting support. Developing self-love.	Emotional and mental: self-expression, asking for help, recognising and loving yourself.
6: Trusting your intuition (chapter 7).	Watching out for stepping-stones, helpful co-incidences, clues and footprints to follow. Recognising help when it arrives.	Mental and spiritual: trusting that it will happen. Strength of will for change.
7: Living with passion and purpose (chapter 8).	Being your best in the world. Taking on board the life lesson. Contemplating your purpose and bigger future. Following your heart.	Spiritual: connection to a wider purpose. Values and ethics. Faith. Inspiration.

Getting Started

So where do you start? People's first instinct is often to do something, anything, to reduce the distress. However, responding effectively when you're off balance is like trying to aim straight while standing on one leg – nigh-on impossible.

If you have been thrown off balance by a big setback or some other negative experience at work, I'd advise standing back and taking stock before you do anything else.

> HR Director Lou says, "You ... have to work it out. The words don't really matter. I think it's the fact that you've thought through what it is that's so important to you. You then know when it's not there, why it's hurting you."

This may seem easier said than done, and certainly, if you've been emotionally affected by events, you may not feel at all like doing it. If that's the case, it's time for a bit of first aid. You have one aim at this point, and that is to recover your balance sufficiently to become more calm and centred – to move from First or Third to Second State in energy terms. If you've been waking up at 3 a.m. on a regular basis worrying about work, you're probably getting rather ragged round the edges.

One frequent consequence of distressing experiences is a constant feeling of anxiety. There is a huge amount of research about the chain reactions which anxiety and fear set up in the body.

Anxiety triggers the release of adrenaline, which in turn triggers the release of steroids used by the body for healing when you've injured yourself. That's fine if they are just preparing you to deal with a one-off incident (e.g. for getting out of the path of a moving truck). However, the continuous release of steroids increases stress in the body and, long term, that's bad news. Although stress is not necessarily a primary cause of illness, research[7] shows that it does exacerbate our existing tendency towards such chronic health problems as cardiovascular disease, digestive problems, bone problems such as osteoporosis, and late-onset diabetes. So the first step back on balance is to start to find ways to reduce the chronic anxiety your circumstances can generate.

So, when you are in Second State, calm and balanced, what keeps you there? Do you have a memory that instantly produces a sense of well-

---

[7] See Nowack, K. M. (1989). Coping style, cognitive hardiness, & health status. Journal of Behavioral Medicine, 12, 145-158.

being? Is there someone whose face, imagined in front of you, brings a smile to your eyes? Does a special place have strong meaning for you? Now is the time to connect with those precious resources.

First Aid For Recovering Your Balance

You might want to record this exercise so that you can listen to it. Otherwise, memorise the simple steps and then do the exercise. Choose a subject on which to focus – a person, a memory or a place – and follow the relevant section below.

Choose a time and place where you won't be disturbed. Sit in your favourite chair, close your eyes, keep them closed for the duration of the exercise. Place your hand on your abdomen, and breathe slowly and deeply in and out several times. You should feel your abdomen rise and fall. If you don't, consciously push your abdomen towards your hand while you breathe in for one or two breaths, to draw breath into your lungs. That alone is a good start and will help restore your balance.

A Special Person

If you have chosen to recall a particular, special person:

- Imagine the person in a favourite setting.

- Picture their face or voice in as much detail as possible.

- Imagine the colour of their eyes, and imagine a smile in them.

- Imagine their hair – its style and colour.

- Picture their nose and chin, and anything else distinctive about their face.

- What are they wearing? Picture that in as much detail as you can.

- When you have a full picture, imagine a really encouraging message you would like from that person right now.

- Imagine them giving you that message with a smile on their face and in their voice.

- Hold the image and the message until you notice yourself calming and smiling. Then, when you're ready, open your eyes.

A Memory

If you have chosen a memory:

with your eyes closed, recall the first thing that comes to mind about this memory.

Now fill in the details:

- When? Where? What was the weather like?

- What sounds do you remember? Hear them as clearly as you can. Call more sounds to mind until you have a complete sound memory.

- Are there particular smells associated with this memory? Bring them to mind.

- How were you feeling; physically, emotionally?

- Hold the memory as fully as you can, until you notice yourself calming and smiling. Then, when you're ready, open your eyes.

A Place

If you have chosen a place:

- Imagine you are standing on the edge of that place.

- Picture what is in front of you: move your thoughts across the picture and fill in the detail.

- What sort of day is it?

- Now imagine yourself walking slowly into the middle of that place. See each step, and notice what changes around you as you move.

- When you reach the middle, look around again, and remember in great detail what makes this place special.

- Hold the memory, and when you are ready, open your eyes.

You can use this quick mini-break any time that anxiety starts to build.

Some More Tools & Techniques

Here are some more basic tools to help you put yourself in Second State, from where you'll be able to respond more effectively to your circumstances. They are:

- relaxation to calm your body and emotions

- meditation to calm your mind

- appreciation to nourish your spirit

Relaxation To Calm Your Body & Emotions

It is difficult to think from a state of tension.

Relaxation Exercise

This simple, universal exercise will reduce tension in your body, and calm your emotions. You might want to record it, or memorise it, before you start. Use it any time you feel tense and anxious.

- Lie on the floor (or on a bed, if getting to the floor is difficult). Place a small cushion under your head. If you are in public and can't lie on the floor, it's still possible to do a modified version of this sitting on a chair with your feet flat on the floor.

- Close your eyes. With your hand on your abdomen, breathe in and out slowly and deeply several times.

- Breathe naturally, and starting with your toes, tighten and relax each part of your body in turn: your feet, calves, thighs, buttocks, abdomen, lower back, shoulders, upper arms, lower arms, hands.

- Now pay attention to your neck and head, consciously relaxing any tension you feel in your neck, jaw, cheeks, eye sockets, temples, scalp.

- By this time, your whole body will be feeling noticeably more relaxed and you'll be emotionally calmer. Stay breathing quietly for a few moments, and when you are ready, have a good, head-to-toe stretch, and open your eyes.

Meditation To Calm Your Mind

Many books have been written about meditation. You'll find my favourites listed in the resources section. For our purposes, meditation is the quiet focus of your mind on a specific thing (a favourite object, your breathing, the view from a window, the unfolding of nature in the wind, a shower, the movement of waves on the shore) that will gradually help to still anxious thoughts and emotions, and allow inspiration to filter in.

Eric Harrison[8] describes meditation as being essentially about relaxing, choosing something for the mind to explore, bringing the mind back when it wanders, and letting go of everything else. When you start you may find you can only stay focused for a few seconds at a time. That's normal. As you keep practising, you'll gradually extend the length of your focus and the depth of calm you feel. You're aiming to create a state of relaxed alertness here. It's important not to fall asleep (though if you do, don't worry – just start again).

Meditation Exercise

Nicholas Janni[9] offers a beautifully simple meditation, which I've adapted here.

- Sit comfortably, with your back supported, on an upright chair. Your feet should be flat on the floor and your hands relaxed in your lap. Close your eyes.

- Start to notice your breathing. Breathe deeply and slowly.

- Now count each in-and-out breath, starting at ten and working down to one. When you

---

[8] See Harrison, Eric, *Teach Yourself to Meditate* p 27, Piatkus

[9] See Janni, Nicholas, *The Practice of Presence* CD, Olivier Mythodrama publishing. Available from www.oliviermythodrama.com

get to one, start again at ten. If you lose count, just start again at ten.

- After a few minutes, open your eyes and gradually come back into your environment. As you gain practice, you can extend the length of your session.

- I recommend that you do this as often as twice a day if you can and also before you embark on some of the exercises you'll find later on. It is particularly helpful when you're feeling anxious.

Appreciation To Nourish Your Spirit

Since the mid-1990s, a growing body of knowledge has demonstrated that positive emotions have a measurable and marked effect on health. Neuroscientist Candace Pert was among the first to trace how the chemicals released by different emotions (negative or positive) directly connect with and affect the organs of the body through myriad neurological pathways[10]. In a quest to understand positive emotion, Professor Martin Seligman has developed a whole positive psychology.[11] His work was begun in response to psychology's

---

[10] Pert, Candace: *Molecules of Emotion,*(Simon & Schuster)

[11] Seligman, Dr Martin: *Authentic Happiness,* Simon & Schuster

focus being exclusively on mental illness, which seemed to him a 'puzzling disappointment'[12] for people wanting to do more than just feel a bit less wretched.

When you need a lift, it's powerful to appreciate what you are glad to have in your life.

> **Appreciation Exercise**
>
> Take a sheet of paper and write down everything you can think of that you love and value, and that makes you feel good. It can be anything from your cat to your kids, from a favourite potted plant to your home, from your favourite place to your favourite person. Be imaginative and creative.
>
> Write a sentence for each thing that comes to mind, e.g. 'I am grateful/thankful/delighted to have (x) in my life'.

When Nothing Seems To Work

I believe this book can help you to get back in balance. If nothing you've read so far has raised your energy at all, then I strongly recommend that you visit your GP for a thorough check up of your physical and mental health. He or she will be able to recommend help and treatment.

---

[12] ibid

Please don't struggle on your own. You'll be better able to benefit from the book with medical support and reassurance.

Summary

- Many circumstances can knock you off balance if they trigger your hot-buttons.

- You may not be able to choose the circumstances but you can choose how you respond.

- You're not alone. Lots of people have been through distressing work experiences and have bounced back, including the people who contributed to this book.

- Restoring balanced energy is your key to recovering your balance. Your Energy State at any time determines how you respond to events and relate to others. Second State energy is the foundation for Presence, when you are in the moment, balanced and at ease.

- The process described in *Recover Your Balance* encompasses four key Energy Dimensions, physical, emotional, mental and spiritual, and helps you work towards recovery on all four levels, working from the most effective Energy State.

- The exercises in this chapter include a memory exercise to calm and centre you, a relaxation exercise, a meditation, and an appreciation exercise to connect you with the people and things that you are glad to have in your life.

- Being off balance is stressful. Don't hesitate to get help from your GP if you need it.

Ann Lewis

CHAPTER TWO

THE DYNAMICS OF DISTRESS

*"I felt assailed, exploited and manipulated, and
had lost all trust in the CEO and the company,
but struggled with knowing I would be letting
the team down by leaving."*
Sarah

How Much Stress Is Too Much?

Being off balance is stressful, whether we
actually admit to feeling stressed or not. In his
book, *La Solution Intérieure* (*The Solution Lies
Within*), Dr Thierry Janssen cites many studies
demonstrating the effect that stress and negative
emotions have on the body. Stress and negative
emotions can interfere both with the way the
body prevents illness, and with the way it heals,
particularly in the case of some cancers[13]. The
idea that stress compromises our immune
response, something which even in the mid
1990s was thought unlikely, is now becoming
widely accepted in the medical profession.

---

[13] See Janssen, Thierry, *La Solution Intérieure*, Fayard
2006, p 87

If you've been living with a stressful situation for more than a few weeks, do consider visiting your GP, who can check your physical state of health and identify any problems. They will suggest ways you can help yourself to lessen both your stress and its effects on you, and encourage you to take some action to move to a more balanced way of life.

What happens next is your choice. It may seem obvious to say that the first step towards recovering your balance is to want to move on. If you are obsessively going over and over negative events, you may still be drawing a strange comfort from such activity, but in the long term, it won't help you. It's important that you accept that what is going on at work is toxic for you, and decide to do something to change it, because you can make that choice.

Choosing to stay stuck puts the control of your emotions and your life somewhere outside you in the external environment – so you're not in charge of your own destiny. It will also continue to allow negative emotions to affect your physical well-being and your performance. However, you are still with me, so I am guessing that you are willing to start getting grounded again, to calm the emotional rollercoaster, and rid yourself of some of the negative effects on your health of being off balance.

Everyone's Experience Is Different

It can take a while from the start of a decline to deciding to take control of the situation. Sometimes this may be down to loyalty to clients and colleagues, even when your own position is severely compromised by remaining in an abusive situation.

Sarah was recruited as Chief Operating Officer to a small start-up company, and also delivered services directly to clients. When after six months her CEO stopped paying her fees due to poor sales figures, she initially agreed to 'lend' the organisation the money owed to her by accepting a delay in its payment.

She says: "When, eight months later, I told the CEO that I needed my unpaid fees, he exploded with rage because he experienced this as making demands rather than offering cooperation. None of the three months' fees were paid. The following month, another month's fee failed to materialise. This turned into two, three and four months' fees unpaid, on top of the original three. I continued to give my best to the company, and knew from clients that I was providing an excellent service, but it was beginning to be clear that the goodwill did not exist to pay my outstanding fees. The CEO accused me of having no team spirit."

> She adds, "I was not commercial enough on my own behalf: I allowed myself to be subjected to financial pressure through emotional blackmail: someone who was clever at manipulating my hot buttons was able to get unjustified sacrifices from me."

Realising that your hot buttons are being pushed is an important start on the journey to recovery. When someone else is deliberately pushing buttons, in a bullying situation for example, it only works to the extent that it challenges your sense of self-worth. Learning as much as you can about yourself will help protect you in the future.

> Sarah stayed in her job for such a long time partly from a sense of not wanting to let the rest of her colleagues down (having been accused of having no team spirit). However, she later realised that their support of her was not as robust as it could have been.
>
> She says: "During the breakdown of this relationship, over a period of six months, I experienced the CEO's manner as undermining and destabilising: I had no certainty at all that I was wanted or needed by him, or the company, despite knowing that clients valued me. I felt that I couldn't do anything right in the eyes of the CEO... I felt unheard and manipulated (especially around the accusation of not being a team player), and increasingly stressed. For the first time in

my 34-year career I was dreading Monday mornings. My motivation remained high in my commitment to the clients and the team, and also to the delivery of a product which I believed in, but I had lost all respect for the CEO and eventually lost hope that I would ever be paid (which had been part of my motivation for staying as long as I did)."

Laura comments: "My recovery was impacted by an ongoing investigation into waiting list management and a National Audit Office (NAO) report, which meant I was in the press again about a year after I had left. Some of that coverage was used by a local politician to stop me getting work on a self-employed basis."

Truus, a senior professional who was bullied, says: "I got a new boss who hadn't chosen me, and he brought in loads of people that he knew, that he liked, and he began a really insidious campaign to undermine me everywhere, absolutely everywhere. He was just horrible. We had to travel together, and he bullied and harassed me. It was so insidious that I didn't see what was happening for quite some time. I suspect other people saw (what was going on), but no-one said anything, and I didn't stand up for myself. He totally wiped out my self-esteem. He wouldn't do anything for me, or find me another job in another division. He just wanted to get rid of me, and I had to fight for my settlement. It took me *years* and years to get over it. I was developing osteoporosis from it."

Upset, Imbalance And Distortion

When you are in the middle of painful experiences deep-seated emotions are stirred, and it is often difficult to see what is really going on. At this level, your relationship to power (your own and that of others over you) can become distorted as you draw your energy inwards, or are panicked into pushing against the situation. I can remember being suspicious of everyone and trusting nobody. Like Karen (see below), I often felt sick. You may have feelings of guilt and worthlessness, or a fear that you may not recover and that you may not be employable again. One of my coaching clients had made a major mistake at work fifteen years earlier and was still allowing this to limit his career choices, believing he could not trust himself. It was only when I asked him what he had achieved in the interim, what he had learned, and whether such a mistake had ever happened again that he realised that his pessimism was out of proportion, and that he had more options than he had allowed himself to consider.

Karen remembers: "I was bullied (I realized later), but was told I was a bully. In the middle of it I felt literally sick (great weight loss programme as I could barely eat!). I have always opposed bullying and felt completely knocked off balance - I had always tried to put people at the centre of my actions. The very strong feelings lasted until I got my coach on board and then I began to be able to see what was happening. The feelings were still strong as I was hit with wave after wave of false accusations about my work quality, etc. It wasn't until I left the situation that I was able to regain my balance."

Lou describes her situation like this:

"Gradually, over time, (the new CEO) was wearing people down and their self-confidence was going. They were beginning to seriously doubt themselves, and these were senior directors who had run the place for years...

"... There's an inbuilt loyalty to your boss, which you really want, and definitely loyalty to the organisation. There's pressure on you to have an income. My family was supportive, but felt if I gave up my job we'd have to leave our home. I live in heaven – I didn't want to move, so I felt I had to stay in this organisation in order to stay in my home. I think this is what a lot of people find – 'in order to maintain my lifestyle, I have got to stay in this job. I can't see any way out of it'. When I talked to others about this, my big problem was 'how do I stay in *my home* and leave this organisation?' And this thinking went on and on, and you just don't know how you can solve one problem and also solve the other."

For Gareth there was the consideration of being able to hold up his head when he walked down the street:

"Some months later one of my client's former directors approached me. I had hung on to the last batch of packaging, manuals etc. for one of the company's products which his new company had taken over. He offered to pay around 10,000 GBP for this work, if I also produced their new stationery, so some of the sting was taken out.

"I paid off all my creditors with this money together with all of my savings. However, as a result, I was investigated by the tax authorities. They asked questions like: 'What happened to this money?', 'Why were you not paid?', 'Why did you pay your creditors when you were owed so much yourself?' I felt I was being kicked when I was down; I resented the insinuations that I was up to something, rather than trying to survive.

"I explained I had to live in this town and walk down the street. It wasn't my creditors' fault that my client hadn't paid me, so why should they suffer? The inspector said it was very unusual, most people would have declared themselves bankrupt or just not paid."

Whether you are worrying about losing people's respect, or struggling with the seemingly impossible choice between leaving your job and leaving your home, or absorbing the projections of a bully, you are likely to be seeing life through a distorting mirror, and your emotional responses will be both exaggerated and off-beam.

Often, your feelings may reflect things that happened much earlier in your life. A client of mine responded furiously when her boss chose not to believe what she was telling him. In a lightbulb moment, she realised that this related to an incident when she was a small child when an aunt punished her severely for something trivial, then fearing her father's reaction, told him she had done something far more serious. Her father believed the aunt, not her, and she was punished again. Her small person's feelings of betrayal and impotent anger were triggered when as an adult she was not believed by her boss. Once she became aware of the link, she could choose a more effective response. While it was hidden, she remained trapped by emotions she did not understand and that no longer served her.

The Turning Point

Things can really move quite fast when you make a commitment to change your circumstances. Allowing the possibility of creating a better situation completely lifts your spirits, and reduces the pressure of negative emotions on your body, mind and spirit. The mind-shift you experience can feel like a sudden ray of sunlight on a wet day. This 'sunlight moment' may be triggered by a specific event which wakes you up to the possibility of a different future, or it may come gradually. Ideally it will be something that begins to restore your sense of proportion.

Sarah's turning point came when, "one of my sons asked me the question that finally made up my mind: 'Why are you still there?' My best answer to that question was 'In case it gets better': at that point I knew it was time to leave!"

Having decided to change her situation, Sarah followed a number of strategies simultaneously to help her to become clear about what she wanted. She says, "Before I took any action I tested my thinking on friends, family, my coach and my professional supervisor to make sure I was being reasonable in my expectations. I sought opportunities to explain to the CEO what I wanted and needed, and how I felt, and to review our relationship and to repair it. I submitted a proposal to him for the gradual repayment of the debt. I used several sessions with my coach to plan my interactions with the CEO and to manage myself more effectively, and I talked extensively to supportive friends and family members to work out action plans, including planning my professional activities for when I left the company. Finally I used the services of my brother-in-law, an employment lawyer, to attempt to negotiate a fee settlement, before resigning when I had explored all avenues of possibility."

Don't Be A Victim

My own trigger was returning from a day away from the office to find that my boss had arbitrarily redistributed a piece of my team's work, in a very public way, implying that we were not capable of doing it. This was several months into the downslide and my response was to resign. However, I left without a strategy and with my self-esteem still in tatters. Were I to revisit that experience now, I would still have decided to go, but I would have made sure that I did not leave at a low point and that I had plans in place for getting proper support. As it was, I experienced a sense of relief at getting out, accompanied by a sense of not being worthy of a job at the same level. I was running away. My energy was stuck in First State and this affected others' view of me. Lou's advice: "Don't leave now. This is not the right time to make a decision about leaving your job, because you'll always regret it and you'll always think 'what could have been different?"' really struck a chord when I heard it over twenty years later.

Looking back, I realise that I spent a lot of time feeling very much a victim (a classic manifestation of First State energy). The Karpman[14] drama triangle, devised by Stephen B. Karpman MD and based on Eric Berne's Transactional Analysis (TA) model[15], is a powerful way of describing the dynamic that can be set up.

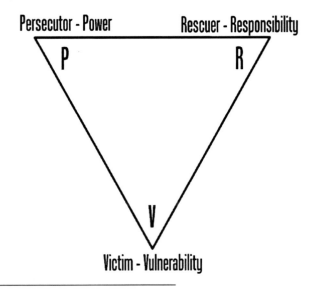

Persecutor - Power   **Rescuer - Responsibility**

P   R

V

Victim - Vulnerability

[14] Karpman drama triangle reproduced with the permission of Stephen B. Karpman PhD

[15] See James, Muriel & Jongeward, Dorothy, *Born to Win*, Da Capo Press, Stewart, Ian & Joines, Vann, *TA Today*, Lifespace publishing, and Hay, Julie, *Working it out at Work*, Sherwood publishing.

Thanks also to Miriam Orriss of Temenos Coaching for her deep knowledge and wisdom on the subject of TA.

From the position of Victim, where you feel vulnerable, you place your adversary in the role of Persecutor, a position of power over you, and you seek a Rescuer to take responsibility for sorting out the situation. This in turn attracts others who may be seeking to cover their own low self-esteem by taking responsibility for other people. By placing both the blame and the responsibility with others, you deny yourself the personal power that you need in order to recover.

While your self-worth is compromised, you are off balance. As you rebuild your self-esteem and begin to work consciously in Second State, you will find that you gain a greater sense of proportion about the situation, and you'll be in a better position to change things. If you take responsibility for yourself, and allow others to do the same, you can be, and can remain on, an equal footing with all those involved. You and only you will be accountable to yourself for your own happiness and well-being. If the pressure in an airliner drops the cabin crew will always tell you to put on your own oxygen mask before helping anyone else. Taking responsibility is your metaphorical oxygen mask.

Now let's do some of the work that will really help you to recover your balance.

Summary

- There is growing evidence that persistent stress can compromise your immune system and slow down healing.

- When your situation arises from others' actions, for example when you are bullied or criticised without inviting it, the other person is projecting their own world view onto you. It is their 'stuff', not yours.

- The negative emotions associated with being off balance can trigger associations with events much earlier in your life. Understanding the links can help you respond with greater awareness.

- Your first step to recovering your balance is to make a commitment to moving on. Making that commitment can begin to lift your spirits.

- By taking responsibility both for your response and for your future, you can avoid becoming a victim and keep and nurture your personal power rather than giving it to others. Your recovery is about fully owning that power, and retrieving your authentic Presence.

CHAPTER THREE

UNDERSTAND WHERE YOU ARE & DECIDE WHERE YOU ARE GOING

*"It was during this walk that from somewhere I got this incredible urge to succeed – I wasn't going to let the b******s win !"*
Rob

Time for you to get busy. By the end of this chapter, you will have a clear idea of what you want to change about your situation, and a much stronger sense of what is actually going on. You will have put the distorting mirror of your off-balance emotions to one side and started to look at things more objectively. You may do this on your own, or preferably with someone neutral who can support you through it.

Taking Charge of Your Self-Esteem

From a position of responsibility let's look in detail at what you want to change about your situation.

This step is potentially a very uplifting one. Not only are you building a strong vision of your own future, you're also accessing and using your creative Second State energy. This is the energy that keeps children endlessly inquisitive and inventive. It is light-hearted and allows the possibility of fun. It is the energy that allows you to respond spontaneously to a glorious day by putting problems aside and going out for a picnic, or a walk, or a game of tennis, or a meal with friends. It's also the energy you bring to work when you are playing to your strengths and doing what comes easily to you, and which others admire.

How you retrieve and use your creativity will depend very much on how you like to express yourself. I've suggested several approaches to the next exercise, but if you don't feel comfortable with metaphorical coloured paper and sticky tape, then do it your own way – make a list, create some goals, or make a plan. It really doesn't matter, as long as it gets you back in touch with what you want.

So, take time to relax and balance your energy again before you start (see Chapter 1), then get out your coloured pencils or your favourite fountain pen, or your paint box, or even your mobile phone, and get cracking.

What Do You Want To Be Different?

As a first step, think about some of these questions:

- Accepting that things are going wrong, what, specifically, do you want to change?
- How do you want to be responding to your circumstances?
- How do you want to be feeling?
- What personal and professional relationships do you want to benefit from your recovering your balance?
- How do you want them to benefit?

Here are some ways you can visualise what you want to change:

- Draw a picture or a cartoon – it doesn't have to be great art, just to show what you want to happen[16]
- Make a collage. Spend some time going through old magazines finding images which will express what you want for the future. Cut them out and assemble them on a big sheet of paper.[17]
- Write a poem, or a letter to yourself, or a letter to a loved one about the changes you want.

---

[16] For inspiration and encouragement about drawing and visual thinking, see http://www.creativityworks.net for articles by cartoonist Martin Shovel.

[17] CreativityWorks are also the inspiration for this suggestion.

Cover everything – your emotions, your health, your sense of yourself – whatever seems relevant. You don't have to send it. Treat it as a commitment to recovering your balance.

- Write a short story about how things will be for you when you are back in balance. A coaching client of mine wrote a story about her ideal working day, and went on to make it far more of a reality.

If these sorts of creative activity don't appeal, find a way that does work for you. This might be writing a list of bullet points on a sheet of paper, creating goals, making a plan or drawing a Mind Map™[18]. Do whatever seems right for you personally.

This is an important step, so make sure you keep anything you produce to refer to later. As you move back to balance it will serve as an inspiration, a map, a guide and a reminder of what you want. You may find yourself wanting to add to it. That's fine – doing so adds to the richness of your vision.

This is how others went about this stage:

---

[18] Mind Mapping was invented by Tony Buzan. See www.buzanworld.com for more information.

Rob got things into perspective and himself back in balance by reviewing everything he had achieved in his role since it began. Rob had been the first person in the role, so he was trailblazing. He says:

"One day I attended a meeting, I can't even remember what about, and I felt completely worthless. I returned to my office and threw my diary at the window in frustration. I left the hospital and went for a long walk ….

"It was during this walk that from somewhere I got this incredible urge to succeed – I wasn't going to let the b******s win! I went back to my office and wrote a report on everything that I had achieved within the previous 12 months, from setting up the service, the number of patient visits that I had achieved and also all the other successes that had occurred as a result of the role. I also highlighted what would have happened if the role hadn't been in place."

Karen also found that, in the long term: "The experience has totally changed my life, in that I got a chance to sit back and evaluate what I really wanted from my life and career, whereas previously I had been on a career path and had never had the time or inclination to question why I was. So from that perspective it has been extremely positive, although I wouldn't wish the experience on anyone."

Notice how Rob in particular went from First State (feeling worthless) through Third ('I wasn't going to let the b******s win') to Second, from which a true assessment of his worth was accessible to him.

Understanding What Is Happening

Now you have a good idea of what you want to change, it is helpful to establish in more detail exactly what is currently happening. Your new vision will have started to restore your sense of perspective and you will now be able to be a little more objective about the present situation. Below you will find more questions to help you work things out. Before you start please go back and prepare yourself by doing the relaxation exercise from Chapter 1 or a meditation or relaxation of your own. It will help if you can be relatively calm for this work. If at any point you start to feel distressed, stop, notice and accept the feelings, then take some deep, calming breaths before you go on, and try to maintain gentle, natural Second State breathing while you think.

Lou's chief executive was retiring and she and her fellow directors, "...recognised things had to change but we were trying to maintain a balance between the old culture (really treating staff well and taking them with you) and a new environment of hard-nosed bankers and financial people, which was the way the organisation was moving."

The new Chief Executive was, "...very much a project manager, never ever having led a team at all. I foresaw a problem because his poor people skills very quickly became apparent. He took great pleasure in dividing and ruling with the management team, right from day one. We were a very close-knit team because we'd had 18 months working closely together with our departing Chief Executive. It was pretty apparent that he was taking likings to some people and dislikes to others. As HR Director I felt my role was to try to get relationships working."

Rebecca says: "I left a job where I had worked for nine years and had always had positive feedback about my performance. My new job seemed similar on the face of it – same sector, similar size company - but the values of the organisation were completely different. It was very macho and the top two senior managers controlled everything. I was angry with myself when I got there as two people had tried to warn me that it was very different and I chose not to listen to them. I found working with the Chief Executive incredibly difficult. He was bullying other directors and managers and apart from the fact I didn't like to see this happening and felt I should try and stop it, I also sensed that it wouldn't be long before I was targeted – and I was right."

Getting Support

You can think alone or with a supporter about what's happening and I'd very much recommend that you do find a supporter. Choose someone neutral – a mentor, a coach or someone else uninvolved, whom you trust – and work through these questions with them. By using a supporter, you will have someone who can help you get events into perspective at a time when it is easy to over-react to everything that happens. When you are stressed it is likely that you will go home and dump your negative feelings on the same person every night. By choosing to work with a supporter outside your home environment you will prevent that toxic energy polluting your home and your relationship. Your bonds with friends and family will suffer less strain than they would if you were making them your only source of support.

Laura called on a range of options: "What was most helpful was having my partner and a group of friends and colleagues who supported me through the whole process... I also had some coaching support paid for by my compromise agreement."

Sue, bullied by her boss who was on the same degree programme as her own partner, felt equally strongly: "Bullying is unacceptable – don't endure it alone. Share your concerns with as many people as possible – someone somewhere will support and help you find the strength to deal with intimidating/harassing behaviour from others in the workplace."

Nicola also sought support to talk things through. "Firstly I used another local director, who was sympathetic but felt powerless to intervene. I then approached my mentor and manager from an earlier post. She was brilliant!

"She was immensely reassuring and practical. She helped me acknowledge that this situation was irretrievable. Together we devised an exit strategy, which was positive for all parties. She also divulged that my boss had behaved like this with female deputies in previous roles."

Karen is aware that those close to us may find it difficult to act neutrally. She cautions: "Watch and listen for a week and work out how many people around you (even loved ones) try to influence you for their own reasons – often motivated by love, sometimes by fear – you might be surprised!"

If you choose to think things through alone, take a sheet of paper, or your *home* computer (using a work machine is not secure or confidential), and just write about it for as long as you feel the urge. Get it all out. Don't stop to read it back, and don't edit it – the intention is not to publish this or even show it to anyone. It's just a way of dumping your feelings safely.

If you don't want to write, try talking into a voice recorder, or go for a country or seaside walk and just talk to yourself. If it makes you feel better, hook up your mobile phone and pretend to be talking on that – the days are long gone when people apparently talking to themselves were considered odd.

Questions For Getting Clear

The aim of this exercise is to get as clear as you can about exactly what is happening to you and what effects that is having. Sometimes it is not easy to see what is happening until you really think it through. Use any of these questions that are helpful. You don't have to do them all.

- How long has the situation been going on?
- When did you first notice it?
- How are you feeling?
- What dominates your thoughts?
- How does this show in your behaviour?
- What happens on a typical day?
- What is your attitude to those around you – your boss, your team, the organisation, your colleagues – and how do you behave with them?
- How is your home life affected?
- What are those close to you telling you?
- Has that changed – this year? Since last year? Recently?
- What are you afraid of?

When you think about work, what happens? Tune in to your physical feelings as you do this part of the exercise. Do specific bits of you hurt? Do you feel sick? Are you hunching over or sinking in your seat? If so, breathe calmly, perhaps go back and do one of the exercises in Chapter 1 to help you balance, and aim to connect in Second State with your Presence.

Rebecca says: "I felt very lost and depressed. I also felt very trapped and my usual approach to life, i.e. making plans and taking action, seemed to drift away from me. The most noticeable problem was how it impacted on the rest of my life; I had no enthusiasm for a social life and I wasn't doing a good job as a parent either."

For Lou there was a critical moment when she decided: "I had to face the way he was treating me. If all of the team were feeling like I felt, then we certainly weren't a team. Some people were starting to back-stab others. He was encouraging lying and mistrust.

"The other thing running alongside of that was the pressure to feel successful in a job and not to leave at a bad time. I've always given people that guidance when they've been really down, 'don't leave now. This is not the right time to make a decision about leaving your job, because you'll always regret it and you'll always wonder what could have been different.' So that was going on in the back of my mind, but I did feel like just walking out ..."

Now You're Clear, What Next?

There are some things you might be able to put into action straight away to help you move on. If your employment rights have been breached consider consulting an employment lawyer as early as you can. If your discussions with your lawyer suggest that you might want to take formal action against your employer, then keep any formal notes you need for that action – your lawyer will tell you what's required, and will advise you whether or not to proceed.

Laura confirms this: "Critically important in my situation was a really excellent employment lawyer who was very straight talking and quite clearly said his job was to get the best deal for me and to be the go between and emotional buffer."

Truus, on the other hand, was advised not to take legal action for the sake of her emotional health. "So, yes, (if it was happening now) I would complain, and I would take the guy to court and sue the socks off him. I did consider it at the time, but my solicitor advised me not to do it because he said 'you're going to sit with this for years and you need to get free of it'."

If you don't want or need to take legal action, then once you are sure you understand, destroy any notes and delete any voice recordings you've made on the way to getting clear. They have served their purpose. Don't keep going over and over them. By all means keep some notes of key insights on which you can base your recovery strategy, but don't keep reliving the emotional rollercoaster. When this happened to me, I wrote it down in detail, and still had all the paperwork several months after I had left the company, even though I did not intend to pursue a legal claim. Believe me, this is not healthy: it saps your energy, pulls you down physically and diverts your focus.

You could keep useful, brief notes under the following headings:

- Your physical reactions to the situation (pains in particular places, hunched shoulders, nervous reactions in your stomach, etc.) I remember vomiting every day before I left for work, a pretty clear sign that my body was reacting to the situation.

- The state of your self-esteem. Gareth, who lost a lot of money when a client went bankrupt, told me, "It was ... a massive burden and I felt both stupid for having let it happen, and angry that someone should have deceived me in this way".

- Flashpoints with your family and friends – what you've become aware of and want to pre-empt if they start to happen again. Remember Rebecca's lack of enthusiasm for a social life, and what she saw as "not doing a good job as a parent".

- How you are feeling about your colleagues, and what you might be assuming that affects or provokes those feelings.

These observations will help remind you what has been happening and as you go along, to change consciously to a calmer, more balanced Energy State.

> Writing things down may also have mutually positive outcomes for you and your organisation, and even prove to be the turning point, as it did for Rob.
>
> He says: "I presented (my report) to my boss for her to use in any way that she saw fit. Whether this document played any part in the decision not to withdraw funding for my role I can't be certain. What I am sure about is how it made me feel about myself. I had achieved a huge amount and in the absence of positive feedback from my boss I was able to give myself a big pat on the back."

Before we move on, take a moment to think about how your emotional energy is at this stage in your journey, and how you are feeling physically. In clarifying what you want, and understanding where you are, you have already taken significant steps towards taking control of the situation. How has that affected your view of things? What are your body and your Energy State telling you about your change of approach? Make some notes to help you chart your progress as you recover your balance.

Summary

- Start your journey by creating a vision of what you want to be different.

- How you create your vision doesn't matter – have fun with it, and keep it to inspire you as you recover your balance.

- When you know what you want, get very clear about what is happening at the moment.

- If you can, find someone neutral to help with this process, to avoid dumping all your negative emotions into your home and family.

- When you are clear, keep only what you need to take you forward (for example notes for your employment lawyer). Destroy any other notes or recordings – they have served their purpose. Repeatedly going over them will nurture the very negative energy you're seeking to leave behind.

- Pay attention to how you're feeling at this stage, notice your Energy State and make some notes to help you keep track of your progress.

Ann Lewis

CHAPTER FOUR

RE-CONNECTING WITH YOURSELF

"...any loss – whether of confidence, status, intimacy, or respect – is a type of bereavement. The same cycles of denial, numbness, guilt, anger, despair, hurt and acceptance apply – but this is not a linear process and the phases will be repeated."
Nicola

Nicola's perception about recovering from loss is very relevant here. It does not happen all in one go. You may have low days, but you're on the way. You know what you want to change and you know what is happening in your current situation. You know it's time to connect with and restore the powerful human being you truly are. In this chapter, you will be focusing on your emotional energy and recreating a strong, positive emotional bond with yourself, and you'll be accessing your authentic Presence.

The purpose now is to build a picture of you, what you stand for, what matters most to you, what motivates you, and how you can best use your talents and abilities. You will think about how you can describe yourself to others in an authentic way which also takes account of their agenda. See more on this in the section on 'Changing Your Message To Suit Your Audience' below. You'll be remembering yourself at your very best, and recalling what helps you to stay balanced and present when you are feeling good about yourself.

When you look at your greatest strengths, successes, achievements and joys then you are defining what you are proud of, and what gives you real self-confidence.

Sarah, who left her business start-up after several months of being bullied by her CEO and not being paid, says of this period: "My coach helped me get clear on what was really going on, what I wanted, the dissonance between my values and the extent to which they were being served, what the possibilities were, how I could address those possibilities – and finally to realise that I did want to leave a company into which I had invested so much in terms of emotion, time, commitment and money."

Karen and her new organisation were a complete mismatch, and as a new director, she quickly found herself out of step with it and out of kilter with herself. She says: "When the first accusations hit I contacted a friend and she recommending seeking coaching help, which I did. This was the most help to me although I did lots of other things to support myself, e.g. massages to reduce stress."

The exercises in this chapter will strengthen your sense of your best self and lay some firm foundations for the future. Stay with them – you really are moving now. Early in our coaching relationship a former client of mine found it hard to name one thing she was proud of. However, she persevered, and found some real insights into her own uniqueness that changed how she saw herself.

What Works Best For You?

First of all, let's unearth some of the ways in which you have coped successfully in the past. Our aim, as time goes on, is to enable you to spend longer in the feelings created by your effective strategies (with your energy in Second State), and less time in crisis mode.

Thinking About When You Are Effective

Think of a time when you were in a difficult situation and you were pleased with the way you coped. Make some notes for yourself about these questions:

- What happened?

- How did you respond?

- What was the result?

- Why did this approach work?

Now think about that situation and remember, as vividly as possible, how you felt about the successful outcome. What would happen if you had a similar outlook towards, and feelings about, your current situation?

What Are Your Values?[19]

According to Lou, "What's ... important is actually thinking through what are my values? Where do I see myself going? What is going to be important to me for the next stage of my life? ...Try and really think through what it is you *want* from life, not what you *need*. What is it that you want to happen? Because everybody needs food and a certain amount of money, but what is it that you want out of life? That allows the flexibility for it to happen in whatever way you can achieve."

Your values underpin your life. They tell you a great deal about who you are and what you need in order to feel fulfilled.

---

[19] Includes some elements from an exercise in Berman-Fortgang, Laura: *Living Your Best Life*, Harper Collins/Thorsons

Identifying Your Values

What words best describe your values: for example, 'integrity', 'family', 'health', 'honesty', 'happiness' and so on?

Make a list of as many as you can think of that matter to you. If you find it hard to get started, try typing 'personal values' into an internet search engine and you'll find lots of helpful sites.

When you have your list, choose the **ten** most important values.

Now reduce this list to **five** and write a paragraph for each one describing why they are important.

Now choose the **two** values you will never compromise and describe why.

How are your values compromised by your current situation?

The Things That Bring You Joy

I strongly believe that happiness doesn't come from outside. You create it internally with your response to what you have and with an attitude of abundance, which brings more of what you value. If you doubt this, just think of all those stories you hear of rich people who are unhappy, or people who are catapulted to fame and who turn to drink and drugs to cope with life. In this next exercise you will be reconnecting with your own natural ability to generate happiness, another manifestation of Second State energy.

Thinking About What Brings You Joy

Think about what you love to do professionally and personally. Write it down.

Think about what you need to be happy and fulfilled.

Think about and write down the most significant or meaningful personal accomplishments in your life.

Think about the things you loved to do as a child or young adult that you remember with pleasure.

What is the one thing that you really want to do that you've somehow never begun? Imagine doing it – create a really vivid picture.

Think also about what things you do symbolically to mark significant occasions.

Truus says: "You need to actually sit down and plan things for you. Little things, even stupid things. Paying the money to have a facial, if that would give you pleasure. Going to a football game if that's the kind of thing that gets you going. You say 'This Is for Me'. I'll tell you what else I do. It's something I did the first time I was made redundant – I bought a beautiful stone and had it set into a white gold 'redundancy ring'. Another friend did redundancy trees. She bought a hedge. It is symbolic, and it's more than symbolic. Every time I look at the ring, I think 'would I rather have this ring or be working at that company right now?' And I think 'No, it's a gorgeous ring – I'd rather have this ring.'"

What could you do that would be a symbolic gesture to mark the solution to your current circumstances?

Identifying Your Strengths

In their book, *Now Discover your Strengths*, Marcus Buckingham and Donald Clifton pull together the results from two million interviews aimed at discovering the nature of human strengths. I agree with them that we perform best if we are able to work to our strengths. Have you ever experienced being in a job where you spent a lot of time fighting to overcome your weaknesses? If so you were probably in the wrong job. Weaknesses may need to be worked on, but only if they get in the way of using your strengths. For example, if you're not a financial wizard you might need to learn about finance if you want to build a business based on your greatest talent. Otherwise, your weaknesses are just a part of what makes you human, and need only acknowledgement. Buckingham and Clifton's book comes with a code which gives you access to an on-line questionnaire that will help you identify your top five strengths. You may find it worth doing to give yourself a more objective picture.[20]

Thinking About Your Strengths

Think about who you naturally are to other people, personally and professionally. Are you a Teacher? Motivator? Nurturer? Fixer? Leader? Adventurer? Gardener? Parent? What else?

What are the qualities you need to express in yourself to feel happy and fulfilled?

What can you do effortlessly, so that you are surprised when others see it as clever, brilliant or something they couldn't do themselves?

---

[20] Buckingham, Marcus & Clifton, Donald, *Now Discover your Strengths*, Free Press

Lou realised that with her family, her strong faith and taking time to learn some new skills, she was equipping herself for a very different future.

"Myers Briggs (MBTI - a personality profiling tool) training helped me concentrate on my preferences and also understand my boss's and why we could not communicate. (We were so different that) it was like talking a foreign language. Combined with working on values, I now find MBTI invaluable in helping people get back to themselves in a non-threatening way.

"So with all of that in place, I started to think very differently about how I could help the organisation and me get out of the situation over the next six months. I started to do Thinking Environment™[21] training and various other courses to build up some skills that I thought would be helpful because I had decided that I wanted to do coaching and development – that was one of the things that really brought it home to me that if I'm not going to have development in my life, then I don't want a job either. I think that going through this bad process at least focused my mind on what it was I did like doing. Once it's not there, you realise that that's what you love to do."

---

[21] See Kline, Nancy, *Time to Think*, Ward Lock, and *More Time to Think,* Fisher King

Changing Your Message To Suit Your Audience

There are two halves to any relationship, and it helps to get a stronger sense of the other person's viewpoint so that you can portray yourself in a way that is meaningful to them. This next exercise develops some muscle for doing this. It will also help you to gauge people you meet and to get a sense of how well you might be able to work together.

When your self-esteem is low you can find yourself trying to be all things to all people, or becoming concerned that you are not as valued or as important as others are. This can result in your hiding your own authenticity in case it isn't acceptable. If you start from the premise that people have different personalities and different viewpoints, your aim becomes finding ways to connect with them from Second State energy, rather than compromising yourself.

In this next exercise, you will imagine you have four different audiences. They're based on four 'types' which reflect different ways of being in the world. They come from the psychologist Carl Jung's work, which underpins many modern personality profiling tools, and you will have met versions of them in your own life. He calls them 'archetypes'. See if you can think of a real human being who might be described in each way – either a public figure or someone you know personally.[22]

The four types are:

The **Ruler** or bringer of order	The **Warrior** or person of action
Positive characteristics include order, analytical ability, authority and practicality.	Positive characteristics include energy, persuasiveness, competitiveness, strong will and inspiration.
Negative characteristics include rigidity and staleness.	Negative characteristics include tyranny, bullying and railroading.
The **Mother** or nurturer	The **Magician** or creator
Positive characteristics include trust, support, help and warmth.	Positive characteristics include enthusiasm, energy and creativity.
Negative characteristics include over-protectiveness and smothering.	Negative characteristics include lack of control and change for the sake of it.

Imagine the sorts of roles to which each of these types might be suited. Some accountants have Ruler characteristics, for example, while entrepreneurs often have strong Warrior tendencies. Teachers and counsellors may tend strongly towards the Mother type, and marketing people are often strong Magicians.

---

[22] See Hill, Gareth, *Masculine & Feminine*, Shambahala & Olivier, Richard, *Inspirational Leadership,* Spiro Press

---

Describing Yourself To Others

First of all think of:

- A successful entrepreneur or politician.
- Someone who excels at making order out of chaos, creating and maintaining systems, maintaining stability.
- An artist, musician, writer or someone else whose creative talent you admire.
- Someone who loves nurturing other people, whether children or adults, and whether at home or at work.

Now, imagine you were going to tell each of these people about you in a way that would interest their particular personality:

- What would you emphasise in each case?
- On what would you place less emphasis?
- Who would be most interested in your particular strengths?
- Who might be least like you?

One more point: while I am asking you to think of how you might describe yourself to different audiences, I am also asking you to consider which relationships work best for you. As Laura says:

"There's a time and a place where you are the best fit... but that can change, so be aware of it and consider how to manage it."

After working through the exercises in this chapter you will be in a stronger connection with your authenticity. Please take a moment to savour your uniqueness and feel its strength. No-one else has your exact qualities, so really appreciate yourself for who you are.

In the next chapter you will use your authenticity as your foundation from which to explore how you can avoid a repeat of this difficult episode in your life.

Summary

- This chapter has been about strengthening your sense of who you are and creating a strong emotional bond with yourself.

- You have thought about your most effective strategies and how they might help you now.

- You are clearer about your values, and about how they might be compromised by your current situation.

- You've identified what brings you joy, and perhaps decided how you will celebrate recovering your balance.

- You know more about your key strengths, and can describe them authentically to different types of people in a meaningful way.

CHAPTER FIVE

REFLECTING FOR THE FUTURE

"I guess it is about which question are you going to ask, and are you going to ask one that moves you forward?"
Truus

Let's re-examine your situation from where you are now. It may already feel different.

As we know, sometimes your best plans go pear-shaped, or you lose your balance and fall. The reasons are many:

- The boss or colleague or team member from hell turns up in your life and things get very personal.

- Your workload becomes too big to handle effectively and your stress levels become unmanageable.

- Your organisation decides to take formal action because your boss believes you are underperforming.

- You are asked to do things that fundamentally challenge your personal integrity, or you witness the activity of a cheating colleague and struggle to know what to do.

- Your biggest client goes bust owing you huge sums of money.

Received wisdom suggests that these experiences are irredeemably bad. However, they often contain valuable learning. You have a choice when negativity turns up in your life – to see it as something to be buried and glossed over, or as an experience from which you can gain deeper understanding about yourself and your relationship with the world. If you consider your experiences from Second State you will be best placed to learn and move on positively.

What have you achieved so far on this journey? To help you move into a stronger space, you've built a clear idea of what has happened and what you want to change. You have a positive sense of yourself, your values and your strengths. You also have a wealth of knowledge at your disposal on which to base your decisions about how you might respond to a similar situation in the future, and the basis for a strong emotional bond with yourself. If you want to keep your balance you'll need to use this knowledge to assess what you would like to do differently to give yourself a good chance of not repeating the pain. Psychotherapists say that high anxiety is experienced as trauma and felt as helplessness. We repeat our traumas, using them to try to resolve our feelings of helplessness – a version of doing the same thing over and over in the hope of achieving a different result. I've certainly found that life has a way of sending me the same challenges until I get the message. So what do you need to learn from this episode in your life?

Remember what I said in the introduction: You are a fully functioning human being who is temporarily off balance. You have some strengths and some weaknesses. Everyone does. You are not unusual. Please treat this chapter as a journey of inquiry from which to gain insights and make grounded decisions, *not* as another opportunity to beat yourself up. It is intended to add to your acceptance of yourself as someone capable of making choices for your own better life. From Second State energy let's look at some positive ways of turning around common responses to disappointment and failure.

Respecting Yourself

Marilee Adams PhD[23] suggests that you can deal with problems more effectively if you adopt the approach of a 'learner' rather than of a 'judger'. I

---

[23] Adams, Marilee, *Change your Questions, Change your Life,* Berrett-Koehler

sometimes ponder how news broadcasts would be transformed if, instead of the newscasters asking "who's to blame?", they asked "what have you learned from this, and what are you doing differently?"

Blame has a negative emotional energy. As soon as you get into a blame mentality, whether towards yourself or someone else, you become disrespectful. You put the person you blame automatically in the wrong, and seek to justify your judgement of them. You also disempower yourself by putting the responsibility on others and not sufficiently acknowledging how you may have contributed to the situation. Notice how different it feels if you start from an attitude of respect, especially for yourself.

If you are blaming yourself, or others, you're in Third State and on the attack. If on the other hand you start from the premise that you did the best you could at the time, then you will be more able to accept your decisions, even if they turned out to be wrong, and to find new ways to respond.

My colleague Ian tells a wonderful story about blame. His job is in leadership development and he has worked hard to take his values into his family life. This includes not looking for someone to blame when things go wrong.

When they were young, his children had a rabbit which frequently went missing from its pen. One day, when he arrived home, he was greeted by a tearful daughter with the news that Rabbit had escaped again. Without thinking, he asked, "Who left the gate open?" His son immediately piped up, "Hey Dad, I thought you were trying to instil a no-blame culture in this family!"

Ian tells the tale ruefully. After all, did knowing who left the gate open add anything to making Rabbit's enclosure more secure?

- What are you blaming yourself for?
- What are you blaming others for?
- How can you move into learning mode?

Taking Responsibility

Lou had been feeling somewhat powerless in response to her new Chief Executive's leadership style. It was when she finally took responsibility for talking to him that she started to see a way forward. She says:

"I think once I'd (talked to him), I started to feel a lot better. I'd started to (express) how I felt, why I felt like it, about my inner values and how I couldn't work like that. I think that started to be the solution for me and I could see a way out."

Truus says of being bullied: "What I allowed this man to do to me (because he couldn't do anything to me that I wouldn't allow) was dreadful, and ... the damage was so severe."

Having struggled to pull herself out of the depression which resulted from the bullying, she vowed that next time things would be different. When another job became redundant, she says:

"I wasn't going to be a victim, so I never said '*they* did this to me'. I was very clear that I had made a choice; very, very clear."

Sarah also changed her emotional perspective over the period before she left her organisation. She says:

"(At my lowest) I felt assailed, exploited and manipulated, and had lost all trust in the CEO and the company, but struggled with knowing I would be letting the team down by leaving.

"Ironically, my confidence grew over the six-month period as I realised how outrageous the CEO's behaviour was and how much value I was delivering to clients. As soon as I left the company I felt liberated and joyful."

One thing that helped Sarah was "time to think things through and realise my personal power". She was fully present as she left this abusive situation.

Lou cautions: "Don't take advice from someone who says, 'well you go in, and you do this and you do that' if you know that's not what you want to do. The trouble is, you're so fragile at that time, you really need people to just allow you to talk it through, so that you can start to build up your confidence."

- If your situation arose again, what would you take responsibility for?
- What would you do that would help restore your self-esteem and re-connect you with your values?
- How soon would you do this?
- What are you allowing others to do to you?
- What would you like to take charge of?
- What is your responsibility?
- What will connect you with your emotional balance?

Asking the Right Questions

Karen says: "From the experience, I hope I have learnt to protect myself and ask more questions. I had been employed to bring about change, but the organisation didn't really want to change as much as I had been briefed to expect and I quickly became 'out of step'. It was a slow moving culture and I had always worked in fast-paced environments, so we were ill-matched."

In a new job, it is easy to take things at face value, even if your instincts are telling you otherwise. Karen initially believed that her organisation really did want change, and was confused and dismayed when her experience and ways of working were aggressively rejected by her employer. She saw them as slow and conservative. They saw her as brash and dangerous.

With hindsight, Gareth wonders about his bankrupt client, "Why had I given them so much credit – why did I not see the risk? ...With hindsight it is difficult to see why. The company had inspired confidence, I was confident at the time myself, business was good generally, I had no real reason to be concerned, or so I thought."

There are often signs to alert you that something is wrong. Gareth's client had previously paid on time, but he realises that payments had dried up some weeks before he understood what was really happening.

If you've been employed to be the expert in your field, do you feel you need to demonstrate that you have all the answers? If so, you might be missing out on others' contributions, and even losing their goodwill. Asking questions with Second State energy is a powerful way to arrive at shared solutions, and it is a strength not a weakness. Marilee Adams[24] suggests that the right questions, framed in a positive way, are the single most effective way to make progress.

---

[24] ibid

- What questions would you ask next time around?
- What instincts will you listen to?
- Who can you trust to let you know when you're straying into needing to supply all the answers?

Being Honest With Yourself

Has insecurity led you to pretend that everything is alright and that you have the solutions, even though you felt out of your depth and unbalanced? Have you been telling yourself that things are OK, even though your gut reactions to the situation have been telling you otherwise? Have you been keeping the situation from your loved ones and 'toughing it out' on your own?

Lou says: "I think that's a dilemma a lot of people have, particularly men, this dilemma of being the breadwinner, being in a job, and 'I've got to deal with this, and don't be silly'. Well, I started to think 'I can't deal with this. I cannot work when my values are being so threatened'."

Sometimes you can lapse into Third State defensiveness without realising it until someone points it out to you. Past experience may have taught you that some key person in your life always expected you to justify yourself, so now you start to do it without thinking. When you are aware of how you're responding you have the choice to do something different. After all, your boss is not your parent or your head teacher.

- Are you putting on a brave face?
- If you find yourself here again, who will you talk to?

Playing To Your Strengths

A good friend of mine is an outstanding presenter and facilitator (a Magician in archetypal terms – see chapter 4). Put her in front of a room full of people and she soon has them eating out of her hand. It's her strength. She will be the first to say, "Please don't talk to me about the detail. If you need that, please ask my administrator". Needless to say, she has a wonderful administrator (archetypal Ruler) who would feel equally out of place on a stage in front of an audience.

Even when you know your strengths, being denied the power of using them can be really traumatic.

Nicola says: "I was assigned a new area of responsibility which did not fit my skill set or personal style. I felt I was being set up to fail in a very public way, and could not work out why... Some of this remains unresolved. Despite many efforts I have not been able to achieve 'completion' even after five years, although I now enjoy great success in a completely new work area."

When I lost my balance, one thing that contributed was doing work which didn't use my best strengths. The job included responsibility for a particular project. My boss wanted me to do it his way. He was an extrovert and I wasn't. So not only was I in the wrong job, I was also trying to do it someone else's way and feeling increasingly stressed and paralysed. The pressure of not fulfilling this part of the job spilled over into the parts that I was managing OK and I felt completely useless. When the crash came, I allowed myself to believe that I was unacceptable to other organisations, and it took me three years to find one that felt right for me, where I could flourish.

Remember my client who was holding himself back because of a huge mistake he had made twelve years earlier? He had allowed this mistake to limit his career choices ever since for fear of repeating himself. We explored what he had achieved in the interim, and how in the light of twelve more years' experience, he would respond differently to a similar set of circumstances. He realised in a sudden 'aha' moment that he had more choice and more to offer than he had allowed. Distorting reality can create a huge barrier.

By now you have a clearer idea of what your strengths are, and can better see how they might fit some organisations well and others not so well. By bringing your strengths into the picture and seeing your full, rounded self, you can avoid feeling that the world will reject you because of this episode in your life.

- How will you use your strengths more fully in future?

Learning From Others

The people who sent me their stories feel their experiences have deep veins of learning in them. Here is some of what they told me:

Karen says: "I have learned what I need to be happy and successful. I hope I would ask more questions if I went back to a corporate career – I now run my own business and work as a consultant – this suits me very well as I need challenges to motivate me. So I hope it would never happen again and I hope I would spot the signs before the situation got out-of-hand and be able to control it better – and I would ring my coach at the first sign of trouble!"

Laura offers these words of advice: "Be true to yourself.

"No matter what job you are in always check your contract carefully, and have a plan of what you would do and who you would contact if the worst happened.

"There is always another life, other things to do and other places to take your skills.

"There's a time and a place where you are the best fit … but that can change so be aware of it and consider how to manage it."

For Lou, "…I suppose I've learned, as I always knew, that honesty's the best thing, with myself as well as with others. That being honest and true to myself, and going the way that I know intuitively feels right.

"If it happened again, I would revisit my values, and not let it get so far before I spoke up. And probably not feel so bad about doing it. I certainly would not be scared now, because I feel justified in what I did. I felt I got the result that I wanted. I did resolve the issue."

Nicola says: "Now I can reflect on this episode with self-awareness, but still with sadness. Getting through it was hard, but getting out was crucial."

Rebecca told me: "I think I would spot the signs a lot earlier and get out of the situation without worrying so much about what people would think of me." Asked what she would share with others, she said emphatically: "Go with your gut feeling, it's usually more telling than any logic!"

Rob adds: "I learned from this experience that I need positive feedback, if I don't get it now I ask for it. I have also learned that highlighting your own successes to your superiors makes you less vulnerable, and having data to back that up is essential in the long term."

Sarah emerged with strong advice:

- "Trust your intuition: if you feel that a situation is wrong, it <u>is</u> wrong for you.
- "Face the facts.
- "Keep a firm grip on your values.
- "Claim what is justifiably yours, even in the face of manipulation or bullying – and keep going.
- "Get as much support as you possibly can to enable you to talk the situation through.
- "Stay focused on what attracted you about the situation in the first place: are you still getting what you want and need? What price are you paying for being there?"

Truus is philosophical: "There's a school of thought that says, 'you choose' (what you get), although I think frequently we don't choose, but what we do choose is what we *do* with whatever we get. And you can just say, 'I'm going to make this the best thing that ever happened to me', and then it is, because our words and our thoughts create our reality."

Gareth has built his life around responding flexibly. "We have always had to adjust to different circumstances and we are not afraid to make changes. We survive by being flexible – that's what life demands."

Summary

- Now that you are more balanced and in touch with yourself, this is your opportunity to reflect on what you can learn from your situation.

- Approach this reflection with Second State energy (Presence), from a learning perspective, respecting yourself and others. Don't blame yourself or anyone else.

- From the perspective of your personal power, determine what is your responsibility and think about how you can more quickly connect with your Presence and sense of self in the future.

- Think about what questions you would ask if things start to go wrong in the future and what signs might alert you to problems.

- Be honest with yourself – don't pretend things are OK when they're not.

- Play to your strengths and look for roles and organisations where your fully rounded self will best fit.

- Learn from others' successful recovery.

Ann Lewis

CHAPTER SIX

MOVING ON

"There is always another life, other things to do and other places to take your skills."
Laura

You are now much clearer about what change you want from your situation and it's time to put your ideas into action. In order to make change happen, you need to let people know your intentions and seek their help and support. This is the true beginning of the next stage of your journey, this time from a place of new understanding and determination.

Take Rob, whose feelings of frustration had been building up over some time. Given a lack of visible support from his boss in the face of cost-cutting which could lose him his job, he felt worthless and deeply unhappy. It was finding the momentum to take action, "not to let the b******s win", which marked the turning point for him.

He says: "Working within the uncertainty became extremely difficult. Whilst I was able to continue to deliver the 'operational' elements of the role the 'strategic' elements were hard to give attention to. The more I thought about them the more I thought 'what's the point?'"

Having decided to take action he wrote his detailed report, setting an approach that he continues to this day. Rob's report writing achieved two things. It was a positive, creative response to a situation in which he had previously felt helpless. It also served to remind him that he had contributed hugely to the well-being of his patients, and to the service for which he worked. From the moment he decided to write it he moved into Second State and was back in charge as far as possible. Ultimately, his part of the service was not cut.

Mapping Your Path

You can treat this stage as though you were planning for a holiday or business trip. When you are travelling you'll decide who is going with you, book tickets and accommodation, make sure your passport and inoculations are up to date and get your visa if you need one. You might buy maps and guide books. You might also talk to other people who have visited your destination and take their experience on board too. Eventually, you will pack your suitcases and set out. You can think of moving on in the same way, and with a sense of self-confidence.

Lou cautions against planning too rigidly. Just as on a journey, you may want flexibility to do something unexpected, she feels the need for "being clear about the sorts of things you want – not so focused that you narrow down your horizons too far, because you've got to be flexible to allow things to come in. That doesn't mean that you don't have some focus, but I'm always worried about saying to people 'you've got to get focused and know where you are going' and I certainly didn't want to be too blinkered in my focusing.

"If you can build a list of things like what you want in your family life, your personal life, what sort of job you want to be doing, then when things turn up you've got a checklist and you can ask 'does it match?' If it doesn't you know 'don't go there'. If it does, then it's worth a try."

- What paths appeal to you?
- What does your thinking about your values and strengths tell you?
- What direction will you take?

Who Will Be With You?

Moving on is much less of a personal burden if you have positive support. Find someone to be your champion and keep you going – someone who can really help you to put your ideas into action and be alongside you as you move on. I suggest that even if you have supportive friends and family, you find someone who can remain detached, staying with you without getting emotionally hooked. If you already have a coach or mentor, that is ideal, but it can be anyone who will challenge and support you.

> My client Karen comments: "Ann was the most help as she had no agenda, we hadn't even met, so I knew she was 'content free'. She would challenge me to look at the situation and rise to it and deal with it with all my strengths. She was kind and empathetic but didn't let that stop her from asking me to work hard, but in a constructive way to deal with the challenges as they arose. She also helped me to stand back from the situation and discover for myself what was going on."

> Lou remembers: "My husband was very good. He pretended to be my boss, so I talked it all through, play-acted and did role-play with him – what were the main points I wanted to get across? And because you're so emotional at that time, it just goes off at tangents, and my husband was brilliant at bringing me back and saying, 'well what point are you trying to make here? Don't keep going off at tangents.' And then he made me write that down."

Sometimes in the thick of things, you may not make best use of your networks. Take some time to consider who might help that you haven't already contacted.

A word to the timid: I have to tell you that this is where my reticence kicked in. An only child, more introvert than extravert, I had always believed I should not bother people, not be a nuisance (another typical First State belief), and I realise that this was still my dominant approach. So at this stage, I still felt that I had to recover professionally on my own and also to keep quiet about what had happened. This had the dual effect of leaving me without detached support, and also of allowing me to stay in victim mode, so my friends and family heard the story *ad nauseam*.

If you are tempted to think you have to get out of your situation alone, please think again. People love to help, and very few will see it as a waste of time. These days I often hear from friends and colleagues who'd like me to talk to someone they know about career choices or sources of information. I'm always happy to talk, whether to people I know or to complete strangers. If you expect people to want to help, the chances are that they will.

> Asked who else might have helped her, Laura says: "Knowing what I now know I think I ought to have seen it coming and protected myself more by being much more proactive in regional networks. Possibly some independent PR support could have helped."

So use your networks. Arrange to meet people who can offer you advice and support, share their experience with you or give you some feedback on your plans.

- Who can help you as you recover your balance?
- When will you speak to them?
- What do you want to tell them? To ask them?

What Do You Want To Take With You?

Sometimes doing something different as an interim step really helps your self-esteem and can give you new tools.

Laura took time off to recover and added to her academic qualifications. She says: "I took three months off immediately after I left and then enrolled for an MSc in Organisational Behaviour whilst taking on a four-day week consultancy job, before becoming self-employed. Doing something academic was a useful focus for me and doing well at it helped my self-esteem. I also decided to do voluntary work and made a conscious decision not to put all my energy into only one thing. I joined a women's learning network, took up running and used some of my payment to fit a fab new bathroom into our home with a jacuzzi bath!"

I found an interim job, and like Laura, signed up for a new management qualification, which I completed over a two-year period. A few months before finishing it I joined my first London employer and was able to make them the subject of my final dissertation.

> Lou developed new skills while she was still in post. She says: "I started building up the skills while I was handing over, during my notice, to prepare myself to leave, and I think I will always carry on advising people not to leave at a low ebb."

- What new skills or learning would be helpful to you?
- If you are changing direction, what do you need that you do not yet have?
- What will you do to research your options?

What Do You Need To Prepare?

It may be that you stay with your current employer. If not, you will probably be applying for new jobs. Have a good look at your CV and make sure that it really represents the best of you. Remember to bring out your strengths, to cover your achievements and to present yourself authentically.

I've seen hundreds of CVs in my life, and if you have been responsible for recruiting staff, you will have too. Give some thought to what works in a CV and what really irritates you. I personally hate the ones that are written in the third person and use a whole string of superlatives in a covering paragraph, but which give me no tangible information from which to judge the subject.

Don't forget that whoever reads your CV may have several hundreds to wade through, and only an hour in which to do it (no, I'm not exaggerating). Be concise, and keep your CV to two sides. It is possible to convey a lot of relevant information in that space, even if you have years of experience. One of my favourite sources of advice on writing CVs is Steve Holmes[25], whose CV Masterclass website includes a range of comprehensive 'how to' guides at a very reasonable price.

Another essential part of your preparation to move on is becoming clear about what you want to say about this episode in your life. I remember going as a candidate to a recruitment agency and feeling really ashamed of what had happened to me. Now, I would be clearer, and would also take time to assess my strengths and potential contribution to a new job, rather than

---

[25] see www.cv-masterclass.com

believing that no-one would want to employ me. Do this piece of thinking in Second State.

> Karen continued to use her coaching experience after she left her organisation. She says: "The coaching structure Ann used with me has proved invaluable – on my first consultancy job I got cold feet at literally the 11th hour and wanted to phone Ann, but thought it would be a bit unfair as it was the middle of the night! So I talked myself through Ann's approach and went to the assignment the next day knowing what I needed to do and how to go about it."
>
> Sarah puts it this way: "I would express my convictions more clearly to other stakeholders (team, non executive directors, etc.) even if they – or others – accused me of being wrong: I would be less concerned with being 100 percent rationally right and more concerned with being morally comfortable. I would know that 'right' means right *for me.*"

- Do you need to update your CV?
- How will you talk about moving on?
- What will you say to yourself as you go forward?

Summary

- Moving on is more easily managed if you have a sense of where you're going. Think about what appeals to you, and what your values and strengths tell you.

- Having someone to support you is really helpful. If you have a coach or mentor, that's great. Otherwise choose someone neutral who can cheer you on. Think about who else can help you recover your balance.

- Plan to gain any new skills you may need.

- Make sure your CV is up to date. Get advice on preparing it professionally.

- Rehearse how you want to present your moving on to other people, and what you want to say to yourself.

CHAPTER SEVEN

MAKING THE MOST OF SYNCHRONICITY & INTUITION

"Things do definitely come. If you believe in them strongly enough and if you put enough energy into believing it will happen, something will turn up. It's thinking positively and being clear about the sorts of things you want."
Lou

If you have a dog you may be so used to its jumping up immediately you think of taking it for a walk that you hardly give it a second thought. Biologist Rupert Sheldrake[26] has meticulously researched telepathy between humans and between humans and animals, providing a wealth of evidence for what he calls our 'seventh sense'. Developing this sense can really help you recover your balance. It shows up in two key ways that matter for us here: through synchronicity and through your intuition.

---

[26] Sheldrake, Rupert, *The Sense of being Stared At*, Random House

So let's look at the balance between the rational thinking that Western culture values most highly, and the more intuitive thinking and connection often described as 'right brain' thinking. If you can make use of both, and set off with a sense of curiosity about what will happen next, fascinating things start to occur.

Choosing Your Beliefs

In his funny, inspiring book about his own recovery from catastrophic business failure and his subsequent journey to success, Adrian Gilpin[27], Chairman of the Institute of Human Development (IHD) in the UK, talks about a point in his life when he decided to stop living from a place of fear and change his beliefs about himself and his experiences. His previous stance had been, "Why me?" coupled with an assumption that at some point, work and money would dry up. Forever. Now he felt free to choose carefully what he would believe about every aspect of his life, and seek out the evidence that supported his belief. I first heard Gilpin speak just as I was about to leave the world of employment for my own business. He is a compelling, gifted speaker and his commitment to help ordinary people become exceptional leaders shines from him.

---

[27] Gilpin, Adrian, *Unstoppable,* Capstone Publishing

Gilpin believes that through our thoughts and our language we create the world. If we expect things to go wrong, they will. If we repeatedly tell someone they are clumsy, they will be. There is research to support his suggestion. Rosenthal and Jacobson's oft-quoted "Pygmalion in the Classroom" [28] study concluded that if teachers were told that students were intellectually gifted, even when objectively they were of average ability, the teachers behaved differently towards them, and their expectations seemed to improve the results of the students concerned. This was among the first of such studies. [29]

Truus says: "I have a choice. I can sit here and worry about (finding work), and live in a world of scarcity, which is uncomfortable, unpleasant and drives me mad. Or I could say: 'The Universe will provide, I don't know how, but I trust it.' Now I'm not sure that either one of those is going to get me work, but I know which one feels better. So that's the world I choose to live in. Now, I'm not in it every day, and I go up and down, and at this time of the year (November) it's tough, but you

---

[28] Rosenthal, R, and Jacobson, L. *Pygmalion in the Classroom: Teacher Expectation and Pupils' Intellectual Development.* New York: Holt, Rinehart and Winston, Inc., 1968.

[29] For a discussion of later findings on the effect of teachers' expectations, see Cotton, K, *Expectations and Student Outcomes* at www.nwrel.org/scpd/sirs/4/cu7.html

have a choice – what are you going to do? Choose the thing that feels better or choose the thing that feels worse? It's a cycle. If you choose the thing that feels worse, you will feel bad. That's guaranteed."

Lou adds: "I think the other thing (that helped) was getting into a cycle of 'it doesn't matter because things will work out. It will come to you.' We'd had some workshops on angels and you start to think, 'there's got to be something there, that if you really believe in it, it'll be OK. It won't matter. It will be OK.' I've got a very strong Christian faith, and that helped as well."

Having written his pivotal report in the face of the threat of job loss, Rob says: "I stayed in that role for 3 years, each year developing the service further. I didn't wait to be threatened with a job loss each year (although it happened) and produced a similar report to the one I had done in the first year."

Whether or not you believe in a universal power or energy, whatever you choose to call it, you may have experienced situations for which you could not immediately find a rational explanation. If you achieve success by setting goals and working towards them, you will know that without the focus of the goal you will achieve less. You may also notice that things seem to come together to make your goal easier to achieve.

Synchronicity

My interim job lasted for just over a year until the new owner of the business, returning from one of his increasingly long lunch breaks in the local wine bar, announced: "Ann, I can't afford to keep you and I'm selling the car tomorrow". I gathered that I was expected to feel sorry about the car.

This time, I picked myself up faster. Falling back on what I knew, I wrote CVs for people for a while, but with my management course nearly complete I was getting restless and ready to go back to a more challenging job. Over the next few months the restlessness grew as I carried on writing CVs to help other people to move on.

One afternoon, on impulse, I bought a copy of *The Guardian* newspaper from our local newsagent. I'm an intermittent newspaper reader at the best of times and I had not bought a newspaper for weeks. As I leafed through the jobs section, an advert leapt from the page. It was a Personnel Manager role for a London-based women's healthcare charity. "That's mine!" I said out loud, without any doubt or hesitation. I put in an application that afternoon, joined them six weeks later, and stayed for five wonderful years.

I offer this as a small example of synchronicity in action. By this I mean that, once you have a clear intention (in my case, to find a challenging job that would use my abilities and my nearly completed qualification), you can help yourself by staying alert to opportunities, chance happenings and little hints that may appear as if from nowhere. Of course, you could say that buying newspapers and reading the jobs pages is a normal part of finding another role. However, I was not yet searching systematically, and buying newspapers is not a habit of mine. What prompted me to buy that particular paper and to notice, among many others, that specific job? What made me so sure that it had my name on it? That is the fun and the magic of synchronicity. So how does it work?

Intention: Creating The Conditions For Synchronicity

Synchronicity relies on a positive mindset, a clear intention about the way you want to be and to live in the world, and being open and alert to possibilities. It also needs a light touch. You cannot force it to happen. Wayne Dyer[30], Deepak Chopra[31] and other writers on synchronicity, draw attention to the different way in which people respond to you when you are connected

---

[30] Dyer, Wayne, *The Power of Intention* Hay House

[31] Chopra, Deepak, *SynchroDestiny* Random House

with what they call 'Intention', and to the myriad chains of events that start to unfold.

As we've already seen, victimhood and negativity both push people away. 'Intention' and an optimistic approach, on the other hand, attract to you people who can help. They're Second State approaches that need you to be present and alert. When you are open to chance meetings, small happenings and hints, they keep turning up. I don't know how many times I have opened a book at just the page that would point me in the right direction.

You can sometimes help the process along by rehearsing the outcome you want in your head. Adrian Gilpin[32] calls this planting the seeds in your subconscious. At one point in his quest for funding, he identified a need to speak to a particular chief executive who had just been appointed. Deciding to take a new approach rather than add to his files full of rejection letters, he imagined, in detail, a conversation with the CEO in question and deliberately did nothing more to create the opportunity for a meeting. A few weeks later, he found himself sitting directly opposite the very person at a formal dinner, set in train a discussion rather than indulging in

---

[32] Gilpin, Adrian, *Unstoppable,* Capstone Publishing

extended small talk, and listened while his new acquaintance fed back to him the conversation he had previously imagined.

The American lawyer and writer Joseph Jaworski[33] tells of his journey towards setting up the American Leadership Forum (ALF), and of the string of events which took him, a step at a time, toward his goal. Early in his quest he was drawn to pick up an article about the quantum physicist David Bohm. Having read every word of the article, he knew, with absolute certainty, that he must speak to Bohm, a man he had never met. He tracked down the scientist immediately, saw him the next day, and the ensuing conversation about the findings from quantum physics on the fundamental connectedness of the universe had a profound influence on his approach to developing ALF, as well as being the first of a network of connections from one key person to the next.

- What coincidences can you recall that have helped you find the right path?
- What is your intention for this new phase in your life?
- Where do you need to focus that intention?

---

[33] Jaworski, Joseph, *Synchronicity – The Inner Path of Leadership*, Berrett-Koehler

Intuition

Chambers' 21st Century Dictionary defines intuition as "the power of understanding or realising something without conscious rational thought or analysis". We all have this power. Some people rely on it as their primary decision-making tool. Others prefer to stick with what they can rationally explain. Yet others will choose intuitively and then rationalise their choice.[34]

Like a muscle, intuition works better if it is developed and trusted. If you choose to use it you will find it valuable in many situations. For example, if you are invited for a job interview do your rational preparation, but when you arrive, open your senses and see what they tell you. How do you feel when you walk through the door? As you move through the building, how do people seem, and what do you sense about the atmosphere? Does it feel right or do you feel unaccountably depressed? Needless to say, being Present is important for this to be effective.

---

[34] For articles, research and interviews on intuition, see the Intuition Network: www.intuition.org

Sarah, whose Chief Executive constantly deflected her attempts to talk to him rationally about the business, knew intuitively that something was wrong, but suppressed that knowledge. She remembers: "My biggest learning was that I should have trusted my intuition from the earliest moments. I should have not made excuses for the non-payment of the first three months' fees and should have trusted my questions to myself about whether a *bona fide* organisation does this kind of thing to a team member".

Some years ago, I went on a week-long voyage on a sail training ship, fulfilling a hankering rooted in childhood games of *Swallows and Amazons*[35]. My husband Peter had intended to wave me off early on Monday morning when we were scheduled to leave. On Sunday evening, our Captain announced that we would be leaving within the hour. Unable to call Peter (we could not use mobile phones on board), I repeatedly sent him the same silent message, "Peter, we're leaving tonight." He says he suddenly felt pulled out of his chair and propelled down to the quayside where he arrived just as we were pulling away. He 'knew' he needed to be on the quayside, but there was nothing rational about that knowledge. His

---

[35] Ransome, Arthur, *Swallows and Amazons*, Jonathan Cape

'rational' information was that we were leaving on Monday. Telepathy meets intuition.

Artists, musicians, writers of fiction all talk about the ideas which come when their mind is still. I believe intuition also comes from that field of information which is available to us if we are open to it. As an engineer with a background as a research scientist, Peter accepts intuition as an integral tool in his necessarily detailed, methodical approach to his work. Even the physicist Sir Isaac Newton said: "No great discovery was ever made without a bold guess".

So when you set out to find your new direction, do it with the support of all the information you can access, including your intuitive powers. If something feels right, allow that feeling. If it feels wrong, avoid it like the plague.

- When have you known something without rational analysis?
- How did you use that knowledge?
- Would you use it differently now? If so, why?

Staying Out Of Your Own Way

By now, you have done a lot of work to repair your battered self-esteem and to reassemble your authentic self from a deeper understanding of your values and strengths. With your intention set and your preparation done, your intuition awake and your senses on the lookout for synchronicities, you have a great storehouse of tools to take you forward.

Stay alert, stay positive, and if you start to dip, remind yourself that you are a fully functioning human being who has been temporarily off balance. You are now recovering your balance, and you are unwilling to allow negative emotions and self-doubt to stand between you and the life you're capable of achieving. You can and will succeed. Pay particular attention to your Energy State as you do this work, and take steps to retrieve your Presence in Second State whenever you need to.

- What will help you to stay positive?
- What action will you take if negativity creeps into your thinking?

Summary

- You can help your rational thinking by developing your 'seventh sense'.

- Research seems to support the idea that your beliefs about the future help shape the reality, whether you see this in terms of setting and working towards a goal or believe in the presence of something bigger than you.

- You can help yourself by staying alert to synchronicity - opportunities, chance happenings and little hints that may appear as if from nowhere. Synchronicity works from positive intention (your vision or goal) and needs a light touch.

- Intuition, knowing without rational analysis, is a skill we all have and use to differing degrees. Developing it can greatly assist decision making.

- Stay positive and develop ways to turn around negative thoughts as they arise.

CHAPTER EIGHT

LIVING WITH PASSION & PURPOSE

*"Through the whole process I have experienced
personal changes which have been hard work,
but I wouldn't have missed them for all the
world as I am now back in charge of my life."*
Karen

What's It All For?

Many people might categorise experiences such
as yours as 'dark nights of the soul'. But after
the darkness comes the dawn. With daybreak,
the path forward emerges. When you were in the
depths of stress it may have been hard at first to
imagine things improving. You had to focus on
making the situation better, and then it started
to happen. It will have been hard at times.

Nicola reflects: "You can't control what happens
to you – illness, accidents, loss – but you can
control how you respond to it. There isn't
necessarily a 'right' or even consistent way to
do this. Sometimes anger, confrontation or
legal action will be appropriate, and for the
same person dealing with the same 'trigger' it
will sometimes mean acknowledging sadness,
resolution or escape from the situation at a
different stage of the process."

The key to living purposefully lies in choosing, moment to moment, where you focus your energy. The two major negative emotions, fear and anger, both carry an energy of their own, which others pick up. Throughout your journey to recover your balance, you have chosen to focus on positive, less stressful and more constructive approaches which can stay with you through your life.

A Sense Of Purpose

With all of this in mind, let's look at what you can do to build and keep your sense of passion and purpose, and to find and embrace the joy in your life.

Sarah is eloquent about purpose in her life: "If I think about what I want to look back on at the end of a day, a week, a year or a lifetime, it always comes back to having made a positive difference to another human being, to have helped them find their own way to a solution they were seeking, a new perspective on their thinking which was more hopeful and constructive than what they already had, a different key to a door into a new, more uplifting way of being.

"That's my purpose: to be an agent of positive change by supporting and stretching others to be who they really are, cut through the pressures of external expectations (which they often internalise), and think in a more authentic and focused way.

"What matters is that I'm honest, deliver on my promises, have compassion, stretch myself so that I'm learning the most I can out of any situation, connecting with people, being acknowledged for whatever contribution I'm making – and of course having fun.

"When I'm living my purpose I know that I'm in line with those values, I feel 'whole' and definitely on track, and my own life is joyful and fulfilling. When I'm not I feel physically uncomfortable at the absence or reduction of integrity, and I know that discomfort affects people round me so that we all live less than our best. As I get older I get more and more courageous about claiming that integrity: the price for not doing so is simply too high."

As you have found your way again, you too have thought about your values, your strengths and what gives you joy. Sarah brings that work into sharp focus. This is your opportunity to understand and choose wholeness, joy, fulfilment and integrity.

- What makes you feel whole and on track?
- What discomforts might hint at the absence or reduction of integrity in your life?

Dreaming, Imagination & Intention

"You see things and you say 'Why?' But I dream things that never were, and I say 'Why not?'" said George Bernard Shaw. Whatever you want to bring into existence in your life starts in your imagination, whether it is changing jobs, looking for a new home, planning a holiday or writing a book. So what would you create in your life if you knew that you can make it happen?

In Chapter 3, you took time to create a vision of how you wanted your situation to be different and what your better future would look like. It was grounded in a detailed assessment of your strengths and values, helping to ensure that it was realistic for you. You can take that same approach to fleshing out your dreams and conjuring up a truly magnificent picture of your potential in life.

With a clearer sense of your potential, and an intention to make it happen, you can start to use your connections, your intuition and the intervention of synchronicity to bring it into being. What starts to turn up? Who appears in your life with just the right resource for your next step? What catches your eye and demands your attention? What lands on your doormat or in your in-box just when you need the information it brings?

Notice also what blocks start to appear. Writer and psychotherapist Deike Begg[36] tells of her search for a new home and of the whole string of mishaps, missed planes, failed meetings and lost directions which prevented her and her husband from moving to Spain, contrasting this to the ease with which their home in Scotland was eventually purchased and the opportunities that appeared once they were there.

> Truus remembers when she left her last organisation, "I read Marilee Adams' book[37] and I was very conscious of the questions I was asking myself, so I started doing things like making my Wonder Web of Possibilities – a sort of mind map of connections for finding work - and I ran workshops for people to try and share knowledge."

Dreams, especially daydreams, leave fertile clues to where your heart wants to take you. Your most precious memories are beacons for what you care most about, and what you most need to nourish your spirit. Meld these together with clear intention and you will create the foundation from which your purposeful life can grow.

---

[36] Begg, Deike, *Synchronicity*, Thorsons

[37] Adams, Marilee, *Change your Questions, Change your Life,* Berrett-Koehler

- What is the stuff of your daydreams?
- What do you intend to bring into your life?
- What synchronicities are occurring to help you?
- What opportunities can you create to bring your purposeful life to you?

Joy, Commitment & Fulfilment

As you become clearer about what life you want to create try getting into the habit of evaluating in Second State everything you do, and everything you consider bringing into your life. How do you feel when you think about it? Does it bring you joy, or does your heart sink? Do you feel good about it, or do you drag your heels and see it as a 'should' or an 'ought to'? Does it use your best strengths, experience and inclinations? Does it stretch you or leave you feeling empty and unfulfilled? Do you need to think differently about it, or are you hanging on when you need to let go and move forward?

Lou says: "Step back a bit and think 'what's important to me?' I'd got to the point where (I understood that) my values were about honesty, with myself, with my family and with my work. Who were the sorts of people I wanted to work with? Trust (was important) – I needed to feel that I could be open, and basically treat people as I wanted to be treated myself." With those values clear, she says: "I'm working for an organisation now, and they love me. To have got that back again is brilliant, and your self-esteem just goes sky high then, and you realise that actually that match works."

Lou's values gave her the foundation to find the joy that had been lost in her old job. She also stayed in her home, which she described in Chapter 2 as 'heaven'.

We often think of commitments as those things that stop us from doing what we would prefer to do. Purposeful commitment is the opposite. It is congruent with your values and following through with it keeps you feeling on track, buoyant and alive.

- What makes your heart sing?
- What commitment do you make to living on purpose?
- What actions does that imply?
- What commitments impede your purpose, joy and fulfilment?
- What will you do about them?

Who Do You Spend Your Time With?

The New York Baptist minister Harry Emerson Fosdick is credited with commenting that: "The world is moving so fast these days that the man who says it can't be done is generally interrupted by someone doing it." The people you gather around you have a profound influence on your ability to be your best self.

In a group of generally supportive people, just one individual whose language is habitually peppered with words like 'stupid', 'ridiculous', 'terrible' and 'awful' can drag down everyone's energy. Please avoid these folk while they choose to live in that mindset – perhaps they should even carry a health warning! If they are your loved ones try not to be drawn into destructively negative exchanges with them and where you can, change the tone of the conversation. Stay in Second State and seek out people who can accept you as the person you are, and who challenge you from a desire to help you see more of who you can be.

> Lou places great value on one network in particular. She says: "I think one of the biggest supports that I got from all this was the female director group that I'm in, having a network of women that I met regularly with – the fact that we had support groups going, that we ran sessions on values, on confidence-

building, on self-esteem, and also about courage and thinking for yourself, actually thinking about what is it that you really want... A great deal of support was from that network and from finding out how my values affected the way I worked."

Nicola adds: "The final learning seems to me that we need *both* internal and external support mechanisms - self-awareness *and* mentoring, for example. One of my favourite quotes is EM Forster's 'only connect' (from *Howard's End*), which seems very applicable here."

In describing her recovery as a young woman from life-threatening illness, Nancy Kline[38] tells how she set out to create a completely positive approach to her healing, with the loving, respectful support of family and close friends. Some friends were gently but firmly excluded if they had doubts about her recovery. This environment of total support created the conditions from which Kline was to recover and develop her Thinking Environment™ method, a framework that has since enabled the development of more holistic approaches to leadership, health care, education and relationships.

---

[38] Kline, Nancy, *Time to Think,* Ward Lock

- Who brings positive and supportive energy into your life?
- Who encourages your development?
- Who is afraid of your changing?
- How will you handle that?

Thinking For Yourself

In her books *Time to Think*[39] and *More Time to Think* [40]Kline describes the extraordinary results that arise when we create an environment in which people can think for themselves, with the quiet attentiveness and respect of those around them. She describes how, when people are respectfully supported to make their own authentic decisions, their capacity to heal, to live fully and to change the world, both as individuals and collectively, are all greatly enhanced. Working in a Thinking Environment™ creates the highest quality outcomes. Listening to each other with respect and without interruption is key to its success. In a Thinking Environment™ everyone matters.

How different is this from the usual run of events? As Sarah intimates, from birth onwards, we are continually defined and re-defined by

[39] Kline, Nancy, *Time to Think,* Ward Lock,

[40] Kline, Nancy, *More Time to Think,* Fisher King Publishing, 2009

those around us. We take on labels: 'clever', 'naughty', 'quiet', 'attention-seeking', 'ugly' which feed back to us a picture of how others decide to see us. We choose our future based on others' sometimes biased advice, get the 'right' qualifications, meet our partners and take on adult roles, 'accountant', 'teacher', 'sales executive', 'administrator', 'director', 'partner', 'parent', all of which create expectations and lay down markers for us and others about who we apparently are.

The downside of this is our tendency to believe to a greater or lesser extent that we *are* the label or the role. At worst, we give over responsibility for ourselves, and our life outcomes, to experts and professionals who may be only too ready to think for us. How much better is it if we take our decisions from a combination of good factual information from the experts, combined with our own inner wisdom, in the full awareness that the responsibility for our life is ours, not theirs?[41]

It sometimes takes a perceptive challenge from someone else to get us started on the journey towards taking charge of our own identity and life's work – of 'thinking for ourselves'. At the selection panel for my coaching diploma course I

---

[41] See Kline, Nancy, *Time to Think,* Ward Lock, p 202

was asked why I needed to hide behind my CV. That stopped me in my tracks. Having met my nemesis twenty years earlier and having since reached the dizzy heights of being a Human Resource Director, I found it hard to let go of this 'proof' that I had some status in the world – after all, it meant I was 'OK'. I can smile at that moment now, but at the time I felt completely lost. How could I let go of my CV? It was me, wasn't it? Answer: 'no', and thank goodness my perceptive tutor asked me that question at that moment, from a place of support and respect.

- Where do you find space and support to think for yourself?
- Who listens to you and affirms you without imposing their agenda?
- How does your CV get in your way?

Developing Your Inner Coach

A lot of advice for specific situations, from sport to presentation skills, can be extended to every aspect of your life. One of my favourites is to develop a helpful internal voice to quieten the nagging critic many of us carry on our shoulder. When your self-esteem is compromised you are far more likely to criticise yourself than to cultivate supportive inner self-talk. Awareness of your Energy State and practice in shifting it into

Second is a good foundation for developing an inner coach.

Tim Gallwey[42] divides that internal dialogue between two voices that he calls 'Self 1' and 'Self 2'. 'Self 1' is the carping censorious voice that doesn't trust us, made up from a plethora of half-absorbed conditioning messages and imposed social strictures. 'Self 2' comes from the sum total of our innate qualities, our wisdom, experience, ability to learn and capacity for change.

As he studied the way he and confident tennis players worked, Gallwey discovered that he and they were not giving themselves blow-by-blow instructions on how to hit the ball as a traditional coach might. They were deciding where they wanted to send the ball and letting it happen. Any analysis took place before or afterwards from a neutral (Second State) mindset.

Richard Olivier and Nicholas Janni[43] talk about the 'inner critic', the 'inner coach'. In *Peak Performance Presentations*, they give powerful exercises for creating an inner coach to counteract your inner critic, however strong the latter is, and for 'summoning' your inner coach

---

[42] Gallwey, W Timothy, *The Inner Game of Work,* Texere

[43] Olivier, Richard & Janni, Nicholas, *Peak Performance Presentations,* Spiro Press

whenever you need it. The result is a more confident presenter who puts energy into engaging his audience rather than worrying about what they might think of him. It is a model that works in many situations, not only in public speaking.

In 2007 I bought a new bicycle. You may think that's too mundane to merit a mention here, but for me it meant re-learning cycling after a scarily long gap. On the day I collected my bike from the shop I couldn't even get on it properly and walked most of the two miles home. That was a humbling experience for someone who grew up on the edge of the English Fens and was practically welded to a bike when I was young.

After some refresher lessons from our local cycle training school, I soon began to get back into the swing of cycling[44]. My trainer was excellent at encouraging my inner coach. He told me the results he wanted, reinforced what I got right, and was firm about some of my dodgy cycling habits without belittling me. So for example, I learned to pat myself on the back every time I stopped the bike before putting my foot on the floor, and simply noticed rather than criticising myself when I took my foot off the pedal while I

---

[44] For information on cycling in the UK, see www.bikeforall.net

was still moving. As a result, stopping safely quickly became a habit.

It is the same with living on purpose. If you are clear about what gives you joy, where your commitment is and what fulfils you, you can trust yourself to recognise the right circumstances when they arise, to do what is right for you, and give yourself positive feedback along the way. This is not to exclude constructive review, which is helpful. There is a huge difference, however, between "I was rubbish at that and I'm a total failure" and "I was pleased with 'x', and I want to do 'y' differently next time".

So listen to what you are saying to yourself as you build your purposeful life. Treat yourself as you would treat others and want them to treat you. Acknowledge and celebrate the wisdom that has brought you to this point, and the experience you can bring to the world.

- What will you do to cultivate your inner coach?
- How will you quieten your negative inner critic?
- How will you encourage constructive feedback for yourself?

"Whatever you can do, or dream you can, begin it. Boldness has genius, power and magic in it." *Goethe*

"Go confidently in the direction of your dreams! Live the life you've imagined. As you simplify your life, the laws of the universe will be simpler." *Henry David Thoreau*

Summary

- Recovering your balance gives you an opportunity to look beyond the day-to-day, to gain a sense of passion and purpose in your life.

- Clues to where your heart wants to take you often emerge from dreaming and imagination, in the same way that you created your vision for recovering your balance. There are clues in your most precious memories, and Intention supports the way forward.

- It helps to get into the habit of evaluating everything you choose to do in terms of how you feel about it, whether it uses your best strengths and if it is aligned with your values.

- Spend time with people who appreciate you for who you are, and try to avoid negative thinkers who drain the energy of those around them.

- Seek out opportunities to think for yourself with people who support and respect your right to do so.

- Develop a strong inner coach to support you. Awareness of your Energy State will support you in this.

Ann Lewis

POSTSCRIPT

"Do I have regrets? No way! The light burns brighter after the darkness. The hardest bit is having the courage and energy to move towards that light when you have been paralysed by fear and insecurity."
Nicola

When *Recover Your Balance* was first published in 2008 (as *Getting Back on Track*), the people who told me their stories were well on the way to recovery. I wanted to know how they were doing in 2010. I contacted all ten of them, and eight responded. They're a testament to the idea that you can recover your balance and thrive again. There is life after bad times at work!

Here's what they told me:

Lou, who had suffered a very difficult new chief executive, says: "I was lucky to be offered a part time role, again in the Charity sector, close to home, after my negative and harmful work experience. I went to the interview, with a *very* clear 'list' of what I needed in an organisation, a boss and a team to work with. This employment proved to be so beneficial in improving both my relationships with others and my self-esteem. I was able to end my working career in an organisation that appreciated its people, employees and all stakeholders. This so boosted my confidence I stayed for five years, and really believe I added value.

"I have now retired from the charity, but have kept on some coaching work, which has enabled me to encourage others to believe in themselves, discover their true values/beliefs and realise their potential. I have five grandchildren under the age of five, which has allowed me to get back to playing and really enjoying my family."

Having resigned from the job in which she had felt so diminished, Sarah revived her own dormant executive coaching company. She has discovered that the more she lives by her own values (holding on to them even in the most challenging situations), the more the company thrives and the easier her work is. Clients and suppliers seem drawn to both the transparency and the integrity, and Sarah finds herself feeling calmer and more peaceful. She now trusts her intuition more and is making tough decisions more easily.

After three years in his last NHS role, Rob made a career change and started working in learning and development. Here he has really found his niche. "I have felt more of a sense of belonging in my current role than I ever have before," he says.

Several years on he is in a management development role and most of his work involves coaching first and second line managers. He feels that his own personal experiences have helped him to be brave in his questioning, to understand the real issues that lay behind performance and motivation problems and to support individuals through periods of crisis.

Truus has built a successful career as a consultant and author. She is a visiting Fellow at one of the UK's top business colleges, and a Fellow of an independent strategy consultancy. She is co-author of a ground-breaking book on building purposeful, self-renewing organisations, published in 2010.

When I spoke with Truus she was in the middle of moving home. "Now my elder children have married, I'm 'rightsizing' my home, my environment and my carbon footprint," she said. "After living in the depths of the English countryside, I'm really looking forward to being able to walk to my local shops and market, and I'll be able to walk to the pub. For the first time in over 25 years I won't have to drive miles to get supplies, and although I'll miss my garden and the views, I certainly won't miss the heating oil bill!"

Rebecca had struggled in a bullying culture she had been warned against. She told me: "My life in the world of work is much improved. After leaving the job which made me miserable I went on to do interim contracts and have ended up working permanently in a job which I love for an organisation which has the same values as me. The good thing is that I know that I would plan my exit strategy more quickly and more confidently if I found myself unhappy at work again."

Karen has also claimed her freedom. She told me, "Once I escaped the company I worked for when I lost my balance, I set up a small business and slowly rebuilt my confidence and self belief. Although the experience haunted me for a while I am glad I went through it, because it has enabled me to get to a new place. Without that experience I would never have had the courage to step off the corporate ladder. As the main income provider for our family, that was scary and it felt a bit ungrateful to have so much opportunity and to walk away from it.

"I handed over the running of the small business to my husband, which allowed *him* to escape from an unfulfilling job. I have been working as an interim and enjoying adding value without so much of the politics! I am able to balance the interim work with my other interests and use it to create a good work-life balance. I had to downsize the car and house etc, but I don't regret that, as time with young children and elderly parents cannot be made up another day! I am hoping to turn to new ways of working over the coming years by developing more of a portfolio career, but who knows? I don't feel stuck or trapped or needing to conform to someone else's view of the world, so overall the experience has been totally liberating."

After being hounded out of her role as an NHS Trust chief executive, Laura spent some time thinking about what she might do next. She tried working in a London consultancy firm but the content of their work wasn't appealing. She then thought some further study might help so had great fun doing an MSc in Organisational Behaviour with a thesis on women's leadership whilst setting up her own business as a leadership coach. She still reflects on how long the recovery took, why she got herself on a single minded track to be a chief executive by the age of 40 and how organisations can nurture their leaders. Most importantly though her work now helps leaders nurture themselves.

Nicola had been frozen out of her job by a bullying boss after successfully holding the fort during her boss's extended holiday. She says: "I've never thought about that time at work without a huge feeling of gratitude at having got out. It feels like escaping from an accident: a car or a plane crash. I don't often have nightmares, but occasional bad dreams put me right back in the situation, feeling responsible but impotent, guilty and very afraid.

"I now have an exceptionally successful freelance business, playing to my strengths as a teacher and mentor to top professionals. This is balanced by using my creative talents: I've just completed a radio play for the BBC, and am in my second year of an arts degree at the Open University.

"Best of all, my personal life has finally been fulfilled by being with the kindest and most loving man possible. I would never have had the time or emotional space to notice him when I was working in that place. Do I have regrets? No way! The light burns brighter after the darkness. The hardest bit is having the courage and energy to move towards that light when you have been paralysed by fear and insecurity."

I think Nicola's final comments say it all. You can do it too.

RESOURCES

Health & Healing

Barrie, Heather, holistic health and wellbeing programmes with email support: *www.harries-food.com*

Harrison, Eric, *Teach Yourself to Meditate*, Piatkus

Harrison, Eric, *How Meditation Heals*, Piatkus

Janssen, Dr Thierry, *La Solution Intérieure*, Fayard. English edition, *The Solution Lies Within*, published June 2010

Nowack, Ken, Research articles on stress: *www.envisiatools.com/researchArticles.asp?prd_shortName=SAP&sideLink=0*

Pert, Dr Candace B, *Molecules of Emotion*, Simon & Schuster

Rushton, AnnA, *How to Cope Successfully with Stress*, Wellhouse Publishing

Seaward, Brian Luke, *Stand Like Mountain, Flow Like Water*, Health Communications Inc.

Taking Back Control

Adams, *Andrea, Bullying at Work – How To Confront And Overcome It*, Virago

Adams, Marilee, *Change your Questions, Change your Life*, Berrett-Koehler

Berman-Fortgang, Laura, *Living your Best Life*, Thorsons

Buckingham, Marcus and Clifton, Donald, *Now Discover Your Strengths*, Free Press

Holmes, Steve, CV Masterclass: *www.cvspecial.co.uk*

Janni, Nicholas, *The Practice of Presence*, CD available from *www.oliviermythodrama.com*

Johnstone, Dr Chris, *Find Your Power*, Nicholas Brealey

Kline, Nancy, *Time to Think – Listening to Ignite the Human Mind*, Ward Lock

Kline, Nancy, *More Time to Think*, Fisher King Publishing

Namie, Gary PhD & Namie, Ruth PhD, *The Bully at Work – What You Can Do to Stop the Hurt and Reclaim Your Dignity on the Job*, Sourcebooks Inc.

Olivier, Richard and Janni, Nicholas, *Peak Performance Presentations – how to present with passion and purpose,* Spiro Press

Rodenburg, Patsy, *Presence – how to use positive energy for success.* (US edition: *The Second Circle*), Penguin

Scott, Dr. Daniel, *Verbal Self Defense in The Workplace*, Bookshaker

Psychology

Babiak, Paul PhD & Hare, Robert PhD, *Snakes in Suits – when psychopaths go to work*, Collins

Casserly, Tim & Megginson, David, *Learning from Burnout – developing sustainable leaders and avoiding career derailment*, Butterworth-Heinemann

Debnam, Susan, *Mine's Bigger than Yours – understanding and handling egos at work*, Marshall Cavendish

Gallwey, W Timothy, *The Inner Game of Work*, Texere

Goleman, Daniel, *Destructive Emotions and how we can overcome them, a dialogue with the Dalai Lama*, Bloomsbury

Hay, Julie, *Working it Out at Work*, Sherwood Publishing

Hill, Gareth, *Masculine & Feminine – the Natural Flow of Opposites in the Psyche*, Shambahala

James, Muriel and Jongeward, Dorothy, *Born to Win*, Da Capo Press

Kroeger, Otto, Theusen, Janet M, *Type Talk*, Dell (Random House)

Kroeger, Otto, Theusen, Janet M & Rutledge, Hile, *Type Talk at Work*, Dell (Random House)

Seligman, Dr Martin, *Authentic Happiness*, (Simon & Schuster)

Stewart, Ian and Joines, Vann, *TA Today*, Lifespace Publishing

Inspiration

Ayot, William, *Small Things that Matter* (poetry), *www.williamayot.com*

Crofts, Neil, *Authentic*, Capstone Publishing

Gilpin, Adrian, *Unstoppable – the pathway to living an inspired life*, Capstone Publishing

Jaworski, Joseph, *Synchronicity – The Inner Path of Leadership*, Berrett-Koehler

Olivier, Richard, *Inspirational Leadership – Henry V & the Muse of Fire*, Spiro Press

Shovel, Martin and Leyton, Martha: *www.creativityworks.net* - creative and visual thinking

The Bigger Picture

Begg, Deike, *Synchronicity*, Thorsons

Chopra, Deepak, *SynchroDestiny*, Random House

Dyer, Dr Wayne, *The Power of Intention*, Hay House

Intuition: articles and interviews with scientists and others, *www.intuition.org*

Laszlo, Ervin, *Science and the Akashic Field*, Inner Traditions, Rochester, Vermont

McTaggart, Lynne, *The Field*, Thorsons Element

Naparstek, Belleruth, *Your Sixth Sense – unlocking the power of your intuition*, HarperCollins

Sheldrake, Rupert, *The Sense of Being Stared At*, Arrow Books

Spencer, Sabina, *The Heart of Leadership*, Random House Rider

Wheatley, Margaret, *Leadership and the New Science* , Berrett-Koehler

Whyte, David, *Crossing the Unknown Sea – Work and the Shaping of Identity*, Penguin

Coaching

To find out more about coaching support and for other resources to help you recover your balance, visit *www.recoveryourbalance.com*

ABOUT ANN LEWIS

Ann became a leadership coach in 2003 after a long career in Human Resources (HR). She is particularly interested in how leaders show up in the world, and how their energy and Presence affect their ability to gain the trust, co-operation and support of those they work with. Her experience of being bullied early in her career and of coaching people who have lost their balance at work have helped her to recognise her own energy challenges and to find effective ways to develop Presence. She has a deep understanding of how important it is for leaders to stay aware of their emotional responses to the ups and downs of their leadership role in order to remain balanced and effective.

Ann is an experienced coach and facilitator, with a Diploma in Advanced Executive Coaching from the Academy of Executive Coaching (AoEC). She is also an AoEC Accredited Professional Executive Coach. She believes passionately that coaching can be a real help both in leadership development and in recovering balance. Her coaching is regularly supervised through the Coaching Supervision Academy.

Ann's HR career started with manufacturing companies including Beecham Pharmaceuticals (now part of Glaxo SmithKline). She later worked for 16 years in the UK charity sector. From 1992 to 2002 she was Director of Human Resources for major charities including the children's helpline ChildLine and the Peabody Trust. She is a Common Purpose graduate, a Chartered Fellow of the CIPD, a Fellow of the Institute of Business Consulting and a member of the Association for Coaching and ANKLe (A New Kind of Leadership).

Ann loves theatre and believes a lot can be learned from how actors prepare and develop their Presence through body awareness and imagination. She now draws on what she has learned over the years especially from performance and voice lessons to support her work with clients. Ann sings in a local choir and used to be involved in amateur drama. (She still can't quite believe that she once played Rosalind in Shakespeare's *As You Like It!*)

Ann is married to Peter, an electronics engineer and lives on the Isle of Wight. As well as singing, she enjoys spending time with friends, walking, photography (she created the photographs for her website), her garden (including the birds and red squirrels) and a little gentle cycling.

For more information about coaching and organisational development with Ann Lewis, visit
www.annlewiscoaching.com
www.recoveryourbalance.com

---

www.bookshaker.com

Align Your Head & Heart To Improve
Performance, Profit and Happiness

BUSINESS HEAD

SPIRITUAL HEART

SHILPA UNALKAT

www.bookshaker.com

**Proven Psychological
Secrets to Help You
Beat The Office Bully**

Dr. Scott's

Verbal
Self
Defense

in

The Workplace

Dr. Daniel Scott

Lightning Source UK Ltd.
Milton Keynes UK
23 May 2010

154588UK00001B/6/P

9 781907 498138